A NEW SENSE OF DESTINY

from ancient symbols

A NEW SENSE OF DESTINY

from ancient symbols

Renewal of vision through the lost language

George W. Fisk

illustrations by
Robert C. Griffith

Cosmic Concepts press®

St. Joseph, Michigan

A NEW SENSE OF DESTINY

Grateful acknowledgment of permission for quotations is given to:
Routledge & Kegan Paul for passages from
THE MARRIAGE OF HEAVEN AND EARTH – *Gregory Szanto*
THE WESTERN WAY – *Caitlin and John Matthews*
RIVER'S WAY – *Arnold Mindell*
WHOLENESS AND THE IMPLICATE ORDER – *David Bohm*
A DICTIONARY OF SYMBOLS – *J. E. Cirlot*

The Scripture quotations contained herein are from the Revised
Standard Version Bible, copyright 1946, 1952, 1971 by the Division
of Christian Education of the National Council of the Churches of
Christ in the USA, and are used by permission.

Library of Congress Cataloging-in-Publication Data
Fisk, George W., 1920 –
    A new sense of destiny: renewal of vision through the lost language /
    George W. Fisk; illustrations by Robert C. Griffith.
128 pp. 22.86 cm.
ISBN 0-9620507-0-9 (pbk.): $14.95
    1. Christian art and symbolism – Medieval, 500-1500 – Themes, motives.
    2. Alchemy. 3. Astrology. I. Title.
N8010.F58 1988
246'.55 – dc19   88-16993

printed and bound in the United States of America

9 8 7 6 5 4 3 2 1

Published by
COSMIC CONCEPTS PRESS
2531 Dover Lane, St. Joseph, Michigan 49085

TABLE OF CONTENTS

A NEW SENSE OF DESTINY

Preface

Why do we need a new sense of destiny? Because the children of the age of science, though brilliantly educated, with more knowledge than ever before at their fingertips through computers, libraries and universities, have lost the sense of the sacredness of life. There is little enduring dynamic in our pursuits; interests are flickering, short-lived. Growing numbers of youth, finding no deeply satisfying existence, tragically opt out through suicide. Far greater numbers simply numb the mind with drugs and endless entertainment. Against a cacophony of screaming commercials, blinking lights telling us what we should eat and wear, our deeper minds cry out, "Is that all there is?"

By contrast modern visitors to the churches of Europe built during the Romanesque and Gothic periods are always astonished at what must have been an enduring dynamic to create these beautiful buildings. Our current generation, which craves instant satisfaction, stands in awe before works which commonly required three generations to achieve. Thousands of peasant laborers worked for decades in dusty stone quarries too hot in summer, frigid in winter, pounding, chiseling, to shape great stones which would one day be lifted into place to be columns or arches of a splendid cathedral. The creations of architects, sculptors and artists, artisans in stained glass, are historical evidence of people, who though illiterate, felt the sacredness of life and lived with a sense of destiny which would endure through a lifetime.

The people of today's world do not need to be building 13th century cathedrals, but we crave for our families a continuing dynamic which will build the kingdom of God on earth, a time of peace with justice, a new flowering of love and light on planet earth. This book seeks to probe the minds of the creative spirits of the Middle Ages and lift up the mental images which empowered their lives. By learning to understand their symbolic language we shall gain a new sense of destiny, and see how our personal roles can be interwoven with the Creator's plans for the cosmos.

Biblical scholarship since the days of the Renaissance has completely lost sight of the interpretation of the four gospels presented in this work. This is in spite of the fact that its exposition had been common knowledge within the Christian church for a thousand years, roughly the period from 500 to 1500 A.D. The substance of this presentation can still be seen in almost all of the larger churches of Europe built during the Romanesque and Gothic periods. It would be a rare church erected between 900 and 1500 A.D. in which one cannot find somewhere the four symbols, man, lion, ox and eagle, representing the four gospels in their substantive style as air, fire, earth and water.

In later centuries when the Renaissance discarded alchemy and astrology as pseudo-science, the Church followed suit by dropping the explanation of the signs as specific energy styles and narrowed the interpretation to think of them as simply alluding to the authorship by the four evangelists. A perfect example of this change is found in the cathedral at Le Puy in central France. Hundreds of years after the original construction a great pulpit was erected around a column in the central nave obscuring the carved figures at the top of the pillar. The vital symbols, which had long spoken an important message to the worshipers, were being covered by an instrumentality for the spoken and written word. This typifies a major change in the manner of communication within the church which was to prove a questionable bargain.

In the times in which we live when science has seen the folly of trying to understand the nature of the universe through studying and describing the smallest units of matter, the reductionist approach, it seems worthwhile to look again to the language of alchemy and astrology. Through their symbolism we have a vocabulary able to capably describe the place of humanity in the midst of all that exists, the holistic approach. Only with a vocabulary capable of expressing relationships between human and divine, the individual and the all, can we hope to renew our sense of destiny.

The book which follows is self-explanatory. Many readers who are acquainted with the rudiments of alchemy and astrology will have no difficulty in accepting its basic concepts. Readers who have delved into holistic interpretations of the universe with humanity's relationships to the weather, the earth and its magnetic fields, sunspots and the solar wind, can also relate to the themes of this book. For those inquiring minds who have not done such studies and feel the necessity for some technical insight may this preface serve as an introduction to the substance of our treatise.

Our most recent studies in physics indicate that the material universe is something other than what it seems to our senses. Matter at its finest stages is solid yet constantly in motion; both particles *and* waves. Furthermore, it seems apparent that every physical object has an energy field giving it both vitality and form such as a leaf, a stone, or a human body. It is now becoming a reasonable surmize that this field may be of a more primary nature than its visible physical substance.

Every human body is made up of innumerable cells each with a characteristic vibration. From the moment of conception in the womb the initial mass of primitive unspecialized cells, blastema, apparently led by some kind of field effect, begins to differentiate into what will become bone, heart, lungs, liver, brains and all the other specialized portions of the human body. Once we have accepted as truth that all matter, all biological forms, come into existence because of a specific characteristic field of energy, the presentation of our thesis becomes acceptable.

In ancient ages untroubled by television, books, radio, newspapers and magazines people spent a lot more of their daily hours looking at one another and engaging in conversation. As a result, alert individuals, those with at least a modicum of empathy, could not help but build up good character judgment and a "common sense" knowledge of the psychology of human relationships. These skills we are losing as passive listeners with too many hours under the influence of the media experts. Also, the people of days of old spent far more time noting the characteristics of the physical environment, the weather, the seasons, the sun, moon, planets and stars. Immersed in this holistic milieu they learned relationships between the character of people and the outward environment; thus, astrology was born. At the same time alchemy, defining people in terms of the natural substances of the earth, provided an easily understood analogy of human psychology.

Borrowing from the teachings of long ago we are suggesting that it can well be true that human characteristics can be divided into four types which were known as air, fire, earth and water. This insight, which comes from alchemy, can be subdivided by the more refined art of astrology into three further categories – air (Gemini, Libra, Aquarius); fire (Aries, Leo, Sagittarius); earth (Taurus, Virgo, Capricorn); and water (Cancer, Scorpio, Pisces).

A NEW SENSE OF DESTINY

Everyone of these four major categories, and twelve specific astrological signs describes a person whose individual vibrations are a recognizable style. For example, an Aries is a person who is a natural leader, an innovator. What we are seeking to put forth in our book is that each individual has a unique vibration or essence which has been accurately described in the lost language of alchemy and astrology. These categories offer a comprehensive description of individual personalities and at the same time offer clues to better understanding of our relationships to each other and the universe in general.

Presenting the core of our thesis, in the days prior to common literacy Christian artists seeking to present the central emphasis of the faith drew a portrait of Christ (a human form of divine fulfillment) surrounded by four symbols (man, lion, ox, and eagle) representing four stepped-down styles of energy. As all individuals were aware of themselves in one of the alchemical styles, air, fire, earth or water they could turn to the New Testament in the Holy Bible where the message of God was created for their specific type of energy as Matthew (air), Mark (fire), Luke (earth), or John (water). Knowing their personal role, they were relieved from the pressure of trying to be all things to all people. What a blessed relief for a rose to learn that its purpose in life is simply to be a beautiful rose and not try to mimic every other flower in the garden. In similar fashion Christians seeking their personal sense of destiny found it in that gospel created in the same energy style as their own.

How did the four gospels come to be written in the unique styles of air, fire, earth and water? Perhaps there are explanations which will some day be found coming from an as yet unexplored cave in the wilderness of Judea. Perhaps there will be another event like the finding of the Dead Sea scrolls or the Nag Hammadi library. Our major evidence confirming the theme of this book is to place a mental overlay of the style of air, fire, earth and water upon Matthew, Mark, Luke and John and note the remarkable synchronicity.

This evidence comes to us in a twofold manner. On the one hand we may exercise our personal reading of the gospels for the confirmation of four alchemical styles in the manner of the presentation of each writer. Matthew reaches the human intelligence; Mark speaks to the dynamic emotions; Luke writes for the "down to earth" daily existence; John appeals to our spiritual depths. Chapters 5, 6, 7, and 8 will detail obvious similarities. Thoughtful readers will find many more.

On the other hand there is the simple fact that for a thousand years of Christian history this symbolism was used by innumerable sculptors and artists in what must have been felt to be an effective means for transmitting the nature of the gospels. The successful communication to the parish through symbols in the earliest Romanesque church caused the Christ surrounded by the four figures to be repeated with ever more beauty and grandeur throughout the late Romanesque and Gothic periods culminating in the well-known figures greeting worshipers as they entered the door at Chartres. At the same time as the beginning of this art work in the churches the identical symbolism was created in thousands of beautifully illuminated manuscripts of which the most famous is The Book of Kells from County Meath, Ireland. Other monks of the islands of Iona and Lindisfarne along with their brothers in European monasteries traced these same symbols in highly characteristic forms to enliven manuscripts during hundreds of years prior to the printing press.

Living in times of international chaos, famine and warfare, when many have lost all hope, there can be a renewal of positive vision with a rediscovery that powerful, individually styled energies have been at work with humanity not only from the time of Christ, but going back to the day of the writing of the prophet Ezekiel, and in religions world-wide from the dawn of recorded history. Such disclosure suggests a pattern of entelechy (moving forward to goals) rather than entropy (a dying out of vital energy). Becoming aware of the destiny which is best for each of us, our maximum energies can be released as we see ourselves as co-workers, co-creators with the totality of the universe, with the divine.

To those seekers for God who have been overwhelmed by the glut of information presented through television, radio, newspapers, magazines and books, it can be a blessed relief to stand back and receive the energy from the representation of Christ surrounded by the four figures. Conceived by devout artists living in those times which Will Durant describes as THE AGE OF FAITH, these ancient sculptured figures will inspire a new sense of destiny for the lost souls of modern times.

A NEW SENSE OF DESTINY

Chapter 1

Vital and Total Perception

Like a blind person... you are walking about in a room which is totally dark. It is a room to which you are a stranger; you have no memory of its contents. Though spacious, it is filled with numerous tables, lamps, chairs, book cases, and odd objects. You painfully bump your knees on sharp woodwork. Your groping arms send lamps and vases crashing to the floor. Fear, frustration, pain, helplessness are your feelings.

How many of us find our life-situation similar to such a floundering, hopeless experience. Perhaps we may think of the awkward blunders we have committed within the home. Our relationships with parents, spouse, or children have been anything but smooth. Or, at the place of our occupation, we seem to needlessly cross swords with angry words among our fellow workers. Even our hours of recreation with family or friends may be more frustration than fun. The worst of this is, that as the years go by, things don't get better. The same painful mistakes in personal relationships go on and on. In our darkness we continue hurting ourselves and others.

We are not so much disturbed by the pains that come with the bumps, but upset by the emotional panic of not knowing where we are going... what may happen next. In the darkness of our situation we cannot seem to relate safely to what is taking place about us. How we wish that somehow the lights might be turned on. How we wish that we might be able to see where we are at and improve the quality of our associations. If you have ever felt like this... read on... there is light to be found.

Too many people are interacting with others as though they were in a totally dark room, when the fact is they are surrounded by brilliant sunshine... only they don't see it. Why? Their family, their education, their society have pictured them in a mental description falling far short of their real abilities. Trying to fulfill what are inadequate images of themselves they fail to know who they really are... why they are here... or what is their purpose in life.

From time to time the greater being within... the immortal soul... cries out against its stifled existence... "Is this all there is?" Somehow there must be larger boundaries, a higher destiny than we have found. Our problem is not lack of light, but rather the blindness of our faculties of perception. All of us have the basic ability to be open-eyed, to truly understand what living is all about, but in our current education we have been taught to use only a small fraction of our actual potential of perception.

Our understanding of what goes on in the human brain during the learning process has been enormously enhanced during the past few decades by the discovery that the thinking process is accompanied by a variety of fluctuations in its electrical fields. An immensely important observation that we have made from brain wave studies is to note that the process of reading from a printed page usually causes our mind to be open to only one, narrow band of perception. As we read our brain waves are vibrating somewhere between 13 and 30 cycles per second... which is known as beta consciousness... but this is far from the full spectrum of mental awareness. It is now apparent that during the past five centuries of widespread reading and education all we have done is worked intensely within that one narrow band of perception.

It is true that through this specific gate of perception... beta consciousness... there have moved extraordinary amounts of information. Since Gutenberg's moveable type printing press of the fifteenth century the number of books available for reading has grown fantastically from year to year. With vast multitudes of books coming into the marketplace mankind left behind the ignorance of the Middle Ages to move into the sharp, bright knowledge of the Renaissance. The wisdom of ancient Greece... Plato, Aristotle, and many other great minds... was published for the public to read. The Protestant Reformation was able to take place because thousands of copies of the Bible were pouring out of the presses and into the hands of common people. With book publishing and ever wider circles of reading among the masses modern science was born and the industrial revolution had its mental stimulation.

Yet, in spite of the enormous amount of material which poured into the mind of humanity through the gate of beta consciousness, this was a questionable bargain. What happened from Gutenberg until today? It is as though in our darkened room a brilliant light was turned on, but fixed to shine only in one little corner. Here, where the light was bright, everyone studied, yet somehow we were still vaguely aware that there were other realms of knowledge not being touched. From time to time we had a restless feeling that vast areas of our personality were being left out of our encounter with life.

Before the advent of reading by the masses the perceptive powers of humanity were not limited to the beta range. Prior to the times of modern science and education the so-called "illiterates" were more widely perceptive than the vast majority of today's "educated" persons. Even now we can study primitives in various parts of the world and note that their vision is more acute, their sense of smell, and hearing, more perceptive. With these sharp sensitivities they can track game through a forest where civilized people would be lost. Not only are their normal senses more acute, their paranormal abilities far exceed our book-learning,

14

beta-consciousness minds. An Australian aborigine "knows" that a kangaroo is beyond the next hill even when it is impossible for him to have any sensual clues. He lives continually in what we from our standpoint call an "altered state of consciousness," but which for him is normal.

It is the growing conviction of students of the mind that even "civilized" persons are capable of similar vital and total perception. Our clumsy and often painful accommodation to the world about us is because we have been trained to learn through only one narrow slot of perception, and have cut ourselves off from our natural, our whole person. To use another figure of speech, modern man's reading skill, working only with beta consciousness, has made him like a knight of old looking through a narrow slit in his visor to see, but encased in armor, he is out of touch with much of the world about him.

From time to time we may be disturbed to hear of "psychics" and "mystics" who on occasion manifest the ability to know what is going on in parts of the world far away. Others may accurately foresee events prior to their happening. Healings of the body sometimes occur which baffle the doctors of medicine. We wonder are there powers of the mind available to all of us which our typical educational process has failed to recognize or train? Can I open wider areas of consciousness which will cause me to move through my daily life with greater sensitivity to others and with better ability to react in ways of harmony and usefulness?

What are the essentials involved in breaking through from school-book beta consciousness to full range seeing? How do we regain a complete manner of perception? In a sense it is simple, something a child can do. Yet, this simplicity can be deceptive. Should I seek to put it in the briefest possible explanation, I would say that this full-range perception, the using of all of our normal and hidden faculties, will be acquired by "relaxed concentration." But much more needs to be said to communicate the mental transformation we are attempting to describe.

Most of the courses teaching greater perception start by seeking to still the physical body and then the mind. Some suggest finding a comfortable position, followed by making our respiration regular and slow. Simply concentrating on the breathing is one way to bring ourselves to a quiet, composed state of being. Some go progressively through the body relaxing muscle after muscle starting with the feet and moving to the head.

Next, and far more difficult to control, is the bringing of our thoughts to the state of a placid pond without one ripple. A child may enter into this state of consciousness without trying. Devout seekers may spend hours a day through years of their lives until they reach this goal. Those who have worked with the instruments used in bio-feedback training soon become aware that true relaxation is not achieved by ordinary "trying." It is absolutely essential that the "trying" to be relaxed be done in a "passive" manner. First efforts at this new type of "tuning" of the mind are usually elusive. However, in time, the mind lets go, and we find we can relax the mental faculties as well as the body.

In this state of quiet relaxation the mind opens doors of perception which have always been there, but for most of us have long lain dormant. Entering this broad spectrum of perception some will begin to have flashes of what it means to be clairvoyant. That is, it becomes possible to "know" events which are happening at a distance. Events anywhere on the globe pertinent to us may appear in our consciousness. In this state our mind may have an extraordinarily clear recall of events from the past. In a light trance we can go back to any day in our lives and recall with amazing detail places, names, colors, odors, sounds and touch.

There is a small but growing evidence that we may even be able to go back in memory to times of previous existence. Also, in such a state we may have precognitive insights. That is, we will clearly see events which have not yet occurred and be amazed at a later date when these occasions unfold before our eyes in complete detail as we had foreseen them. Such new abilities are only of secondary importance. Of much greater concern will be the acquisition of a deeper understanding of the mind and emotions of others. We will have more sympathy, more kindness, more love for all those with whom our lives are in contact. Regarding what is most worthwhile the Apostle Paul reminded us, "If I have prophetic powers, and understand all mysteries and all knowledge, and if I have all faith, so as to remove mountains, but have not love, I am nothing."[1] We should not crave the vanity of psychic powers... a personal ego-trip... but a sincere love which incorporates the warmth of the heart as well as the clarity of the mind.

Not only will our communication system with others be more open and aware, but our ability to help and heal with prayer thoughts will be enlivened. Both by touch, and by sending our thoughts, we will be able to lift the quality of minds and hearts both near and far. Looking back to our previous style of living we shall regret those years when we lived as though we were ancient mummies encased in yards and yards of muslin out of touch with those about us. With every discovery of new and better levels of being, we shall want to go further wondering what lies beyond each new horizon.

This book is being written for those who have started on the long search, who have found themselves somewhat more sensitive and are eager to go further. For a major part of our journey we are going back to the times before reading became a popular exercise for the masses. We shall find that in those days manners of perception were more open and sensitive than they are in the "educated" world of today.

Specifically we will explore the unusually wide and powerful band of perception which enabled the creation of the Romanesque and Gothic cathedrals in the period from the ninth through the thirteenth centuries. It was only through vivid and total perception that these unique masterpieces of man's worship of God were created. Long after their construction these great churches and cathedrals were maintained and improved because of their remarkable power to speak to a wide range of perceptive abilities. We shall see how the uneducated "common" people enjoyed glorious experiences which have largely been denied worshipers in our scientific, but restricted "beta-conscious" minds of the present times.

Specifically we shall demonstrate how the marvelous designers of the Romanesque and Gothic cathedrals used their skills in all of the arts to tune human beings on earth to experience a foretaste of the joys of the heavenly planes. Living in times when printed Bibles were not available we will see how the parishioners walking about in the cathedrals had all of the major Bible characters and their stories clearly presented to them. In the time of the building of the European cathedrals some thousand to eight hundred years ago worshipers were far better informed on the contents of the Holy Bible than the average Christian of today. Not only did the people of old know the facts of the stories better, but more importantly they tended to experience them with fullness of feeling. The Bible characters appearing in woodcarvings, paintings, stained glass and sculpture in stone were both portrayed and admired with deep sensitivity. The effect upon human hearts and souls was profound, not casual and superficial as is too often true today.

We are going to show how the pre-literate people were in many ways more aware of the fullness and intensity of life than we today who can find only a shallow semblance of existence watching the video-screen while our VCR plays old movies. We shall suggest practical ways by which we can reopen doors of perception which have too long been closed. Through this accomplishment it will be our hope to lead our readers into an enrichment of their understanding of themselves, their relationships with each other and to the total universe in which we live. May we thus acquire a new sense of destiny.

A NEW SENSE OF DESTINY

Chapter 2

The Written Word only a Gate to Reality

Before continuing with our book it is absolutely vital that we have a common understanding of some basic assumptions. Since the initial discovery and use of written languages mankind has falsely assumed that the patching together of certain words constitutes knowledge. Since the days of printing and mass reading this approach to wisdom has more deeply taken root. The final hurdle of the commonly used educational process involves passing examinations and writing papers. Properly accomplished this presumes the attainment of wisdom, permits graduation to higher levels and ultimately giving of degrees. The facts of life in the real world often quickly demolish the presumptions of this learning process. Brilliant students may become mediocre in life vocations. Average students may surprisingly rise to the top in their occupations. It is necessary that we evaluate the psychological processes of writing and reading.

Skilled use of words can promote the clarification of ideas. At the same time it should be said that a word is nothing more than an indicator of a thing or an idea. To put this as simply as possible... the word "god" is neither a god, nor the God... any more than the word "fence-post" is a fence-post. What are written words? They are a code used to try to represent a picture existing in the writer's mind. The beginning of all languages was simply picture drawing of people or things, hieroglyphs. With highly developed intricacies of thought it continues today as a beautiful, useful process. But let's take an inner look at what actually happens in the use of language.

An architect sees in his mind's eye a building he would like to create. Then it is his task to make a drawing and blueprints which will enable someone else, a contractor, to create the physical reality which began as a vision in the architect's mind. We follow an identical process in all writing and reading. Authors visualize in their minds a series of events or acts of people, then they reduce to words what has been the substance of their mental vision. However, the created book is only an inert object, of no worth whatsoever, as long as it lies closed on a shelf. It only becomes of value as readers take it down, open the pages and relive the author's thoughts.

We must realize that the readers have a great deal depending upon them. They look at the code... the letters, the words... and to the ability of their imagination reconstruct the original vision of the author. It is more than probable that most readers fail to see the fullness of what the author saw in imagination. Perhaps a few readers with rare insight visualize more than the author imagined. In both cases we wish to point out that the reality, the vision, is not the words, the code; the reality was firstly, the original vision in the author's mind, and secondly, the vision which occurred in the mind of the reader. Our point is obvious, written words are not reality... only seeking to be descriptive of it. The things themselves, a dog, a house, a man, a tree, these are the basic reality. What then are words? They should be described as a "code" whereby the picture in the mind of the author will hopefully be recreated as an image in the mind of the reader.

On the whole we have underestimated the importance of the imaginative faculties of the readers in the transfer of knowledge through books. A major thrust of this writing is to heighten the ability of readers to make the most out of the books... to come closer to recreating the original vision of the author. Modern education has tended to ignore this significant portion of the communication process.

Faber Birren, the world's leading authority on color, gives a fascinating note on this subject lending credence to our thoughts. In his book, COLOR PSYCHOLOGY AND COLOR THERAPY, he states... "With reference to after-images, hypnotized subjects have been asked to concentrate upon color stimuli which had no literal existence. Though their eyes actually saw nothing, color experiences were noted. The subjects "saw" complimentary afterimages despite the fact that the retinas of their eyes had not been excited."[2] For each of us it is these mentally-created pictures appearing before the inner-mind which are our reality.

To make the best use of books we need to read more slowly. We need to let ourselves become more involved in the imaginative process; sensing the light and shade in the scenes, the infinite variety of colors, the sounds, the ticking of a clock, the thunder and lightning of a moving storm. Let us involve the entire perceptive process, tasting the wine, feeling the earth, smelling the rare odors. Involving the senses will help to open more widely the gates of perception. An EEG brain scan of such an involved reader will look quite different from that of an average person scanning the identical lines on the page. The highly imaginative person will develop more powerful brain waves going into alpha and theta ranges.

If we learn to read in this deeper manner, our reading will become more enjoyable; our thoughts will become more constructive and most importantly, we will sense ourselves becoming whole persons. The light which was working in only a corner of our mind will begin to flood not only mind, but also heart and senses. Reading great books and noble poetry will cause us to feel vibrations moving through our entire being as we begin to grasp all the shades of meaning, the hopes and joys, the sorrows and pains intended by the author. Now we are not just reading, we are living again the experience of the writer.

To gain a revival of the true potential of the communication process let us turn to the "lost language," that marvelous, colorful stream of symbolism which existed in the days prior to modern literacy. In the cathedrals and smaller churches of Europe built before the time of Gutenberg and the beginnings of printing in the fifteenth century, not only the educated, but also the masses, were communicating with a language built upon a rich array of symbols presented in architecture, sculpture, stained glass and painting. Within the Romanesque and Gothic cathedrals worshipers enjoyed deep, fulfilling perceptions of the stories of the Bible, the heroes and saints of the church, the plan of faith, and their personal place in God's universe. Living in times of mystery and awe, when their religion involved the entire person, these ancients have something to say to the people of modern times whose souls have been starved on a thin gruel of rationalism and behaviorism.

Rodney Collin in THE THEORY OF CELESTIAL INFLUENCE prepares us to understand the efficacy by which the cathedral was communicating with our inner vision. "Certain of the Gothic cathedrals are complete models of the universe, whereas a modern planetarium, for all its beauty, knowledge and accuracy, is not. For the latter model completely omits man. The difference, of course, lies in the fact that the cathedrals, directly or indirectly, were designed by men who belonged to schools for the achievement of higher states of consciousness, and had the advantage of experience gained in such schools; whereas the designers of the planetarium are scientists and technicians, clever and qualified enough in their field, but claiming no particular knowledge of the potentialities of the human machine with which they have to work."[3]

A NEW SENSE OF DESTINY

Some of the symbols of old are still with us today and so much a part of our thinking they require little or no interpretation. These are such things as the most obvious line of a church, a steeple, depicting humanity's upward thrust to God in prayer. The cross symbolizes the greatness of God's love as Christ is crucified. The water of the baptismal font brings the blessing of the Holy Spirit. The communion table signifies Christ's last supper with his disciples and our opportunity to be a part of that fellowship today. The lectern with the Holy Bible is the place for reading aloud the word of God. The pulpit with its preacher offers a place for expressing the eternal message in contemporary terms. These simple symbols surviving the centuries speak to us today from churches of many denominations. Nevertheless, these well known signs represent only the beginning, the merest ABC's of an eloquent language once known by all, today largely forgotten.

As one who has wandered across the face of Europe several times photographing the churches in all their beauty and color, and later trying to present their meaning to contemporary Americans, it gradually became clear to me that in addition to the basic symbols already mentioned, the churches of old were speaking eloquently to their day in a language which has become almost totally obscure in current times. Their vernacular was presented in the rich symbolism of alchemy and astrology. It appears frequently and vigorously in various kinds of art work both inside and outside the cathedrals. These symbols are not mere adornment, some hazy embellishment, but rather an expressive means of communication with power far beyond the written word.

Today we may think of alchemy as the attempt of fools to turn base metals into gold. If so, we should learn that it was more concerned with turning the baseness of human nature, its sinfulness, into the gold of noble character. If astrology conjures up visions of greedy charlatans selling false prophecies to the gullible, then change that image to the attempts by earnest seerers to relate the experiences of everyday to the vast machinery of the entire cosmos; as above, in the heavens, so below, on earth. When those colorful, ancient arts were lost, replaced by modern scientific chemistry and astronomy, the public gradually became deprived of a vast lore of mental pictures which for centuries had long succeeded in conveying the meaning of relationships between humans and their universe.

In days of old when you said that a person was an "airy" type, and specifically a Gemini, a Libra, or an Aquarian, you were giving a precise mental picture filled with color and overtones which spoke with vitality and meaning to the listener. In today's world this language has been almost lost. I walked dozens of times through the great churches of Europe totally failing to understand the ancient symbolic language. But the power of the signs coming at my eyes again and again made me realize that there were messages here to be read. As the once obscure meanings began to unfold there dawned on my consciousness a new appreciation of the mental skills of the pre-literate world. These people of old, far from being unintelligent, were dealing creatively with sharp, powerful tools of communication.

Of far more significance than proving that the ancients were considerably brighter than we had thought will be the fact that with rediscovering their means of communication we of today shall enjoy better skills for understanding ourselves. Students of the human mind, and working psychologists, are rediscovering not only the extraordinary importance of symbols but also their value in the explanation of dreams. The interpretation of the venerable symbols from alchemy and astrology can afford new clarity for knowing ourselves. In our dreams at night many times we are working out problems encountered during the day. In our dreams we are sometimes open to the thoughts and prayers of loved ones who are trying to reach our minds. It may be possible that our dreams offer a channel for those who have passed on to reach us. Robert Blair Kaiser writing in PSYCHOLOGY TODAY states, "We don't make our dreams, our dreams make us."[4]

If symbols can direct us from dreams, if they are a directing power floating up from the subconscious, we do well to learn all that we can about what they are saying. Quoting from J. E. Cirlot's DICTIONARY OF SYM-BOLS... "Jung uses the word 'archetype' to designate those universal symbols which possess the greatest constancy and efficiency, the greatest potentiality for psychic evolution, and which point away from the inferior to the superior. In ON PSYCHIC ENERGY, he specifically says; 'The psychological mechanism that transforms energy is the symbol.' "[5]

Renewed use of the lost language of symbolism can widen our bands of perception. It can be the path on which we move from a reductionist to a holistic interpretation of ourselves and those about us. The symbols we see in our minds' eye are important highway signs guiding our progress. May we continue on this open pathway, wisely marked, as we learn a new sense of destiny, how to fulfill our special place in God's universe.

A NEW SENSE OF DESTINY

Chapter 3

Symbols Have Creative Power

In the time before the common use of books pictorial representations gave both force and direction to the expression of human behavior. With the development of religion, mythology, alchemy and astrology a potent language was created allowing individuals to communicate in terms of the whole person, right and left brain, conscious and subconscious. This power of symbols to create identity and give purpose for living has been well expressed by Gregory Szanto. "The symbols used in Astrology are a door to get through to the unconscious, inner world. They are taken from mythology and have tremendous power because their images have been built up telesmatically by generations of minds over thousands of years. In themselves the symbols are nothing. It is the force behind them that counts."[6]

Proof that the lost language had immense power to improve human behavior is ably shown in this brief story told by A.N. Didron in his CHRISTIAN ICONOGRAPHY. Going back to the beginning of the fifth century he quotes St. Paulinus, Bishop of Nola, giving his reasons for having put pictures in the basilica of St. Felix. "Among the crowds attracted hither by the fame of St. Felix, there are peasants recently converted, who cannot read, and who, before embracing the faith of Christ, had long been the slaves of profane usages, and had obeyed their senses as gods. They arrive here from afar, and from all parts of the country. Glowing with faith, they despise the chilling frosts; they pass the entire night in joyous watchings; they drive away slumber by gaiety, and darkness by torches. But they mingle festivities with their prayers, and, after singing hymns to God, abandon themselves to good cheer; they joyously stain with odoriferous wine the tombs of the Saints. They sing in the midst of their cups, and by their drunken lips, the demon insults St. Felix. I have therefore, thought it expedient to enliven with paintings the entire habitation of the Holy Saint. Images thus traced and coloured will perhaps inspire those rude minds with astonishment. Inscriptions are placed above the pictures, in order that the letter may explain what the hand has depicted. While showing them to each other, and reading thus by turns these pictured objects, they do not think of eating until later than before – their eyes aid them to endure fasting. Painting beguiles their hunger, better habits govern these wondering men, and studying holy histories, chastity and virtue are engendered by such examples of piety. These sober gazers are intoxicated with excitement, though they have ceased to indulge in wine. A great part of the time being spent in looking at these pictures, they drink much less, for there remain only a few short minutes for their repast."[7]

Having seen such effective use of simple paintings to enhance the faith of the illiterate public it was wise of the church leaders to employ artisans, artists and sculptors to in every way possible use the visual surfaces of the churches and cathedrals to communicate the stories and power of the faith. What was discovered and practiced from the earliest Christian centuries was acknowledged fact as St. John Damascenus would write in the 8th century. "Images open the heart and awake the intellect, and, in a marvelous and indescribable manner, engage us to imitate the persons they represent."[8]

This type of communication typically engaged the entire person, involving not only the mind, but also the heart, the emotions, resulting in a total change of manner and style of life. As Didron would remark… "A sculptured arch in the porch of a church, or an historical glass painting in the nave presented the ignorant with a lesson, the believer with a sermon, – a lesson and a sermon which reached the heart through the eyes instead of entering at the ears. The impression, besides, was infinitely deeper; for it is acknowledged, that a picture sways the soul far more powerfully than any discourse or description in words."[9]

It would be grave injustice to the power of God working upon humanity to suggest that the pictorial language used by the earliest Christians writing in the catacombs, flourishing through long centuries, and finally blossoming forth in greatest majesty in the cathedrals of the Middle Ages lacked precursors prior to the time of Christ. While many examples could be found from cultures all over the world I would like to suggest that one of the deepest mines of symbolic study of struggling humanity in the hands of God is seen in the study of medieval alchemy. Rooted in ancient Egypt, where it was known as the Hermetic art, transplanted to the Hellenistic world, rediscovered by the Islamic Arabs, its language of symbols is deeply intertwined with that of Christianity. This is more than just coincidence, or a simple handing of knowledge from one generation to the next. This symbolic language has remained alive because its pictures have faithfully explained the deep realities of human behavior. The sins and evils, the joys and triumphs, the jealousies and hatreds, the friendships and loves, the growth and decay of human personality... these all are explained in knowledgeable fashion through this symbolic art from time immemorial to the children of each new decade.

Alchemy is far more than primitive chemistry. Literally it means, the transmutation. Traditionally it was concerned with transmuting base metals into higher forms, such as lead into gold. A major concern was to find a universal solvent. One elusive goal was the search for an elixir of life which would make old lives young again. While these goals are not to be denied, it is more importantly true that the philosophers used the language of alchemy to describe the transmutation of the rawest human flesh into the highest spiritual beings. At its finest, alchemy writing in symbolic language, concerned the most important insights of both philosophy and religion. At those times when the pages of history were bloodied by the conflicts of intolerant persecution the language of alchemy provided an esoteric screen behind which the wise could continue their work.

Broadly speaking the alchemists dealt with "earth," "water," and "air." All of these could be affected by the energizing of "fire." Common metals were characterized by planetary names. Saturn, lead; Jupiter, tin; Mars, iron; Sun, gold; Venus, copper; Mercury, quicksilver; and Moon, silver. As they studied the qualities of physical substances in the world about them, it seemed obvious that similar characteristics existed in the psychological makeup of the various individuals of the human race. Even today with no knowledge of the subject it is easy to understand when we say that someone is an "earthy" type person. It is saying that this person must have "hands on" in the material world creating food, housing, clothing, always enjoying beauty in expression. An "airy" mind suggests the drive of a mind which goes with abandon from subject to subject seeking to satisfy intellectual curiosity. A "watery" person intuitively seeks to relate "hunches" with the facts, only satisfied when feelings and mind integrate. The "fiery" personality needs no further description. To those steeped in the knowledge of alchemy it seemed obvious that while the four gospels in the New Testament all described Christ nevertheless each author wrote in a characteristic style. Matthew = air, Mark = fire, Luke = earth, and John = water. We shall develop these insights in detail in future chapters.

A NEW SENSE OF DESTINY

Chapter 4

What Message Do the Symbols Communicate?

Across the centuries of human history certain key personalities have developed unique thoughts and styles which have influenced thousands through the generations which have followed them. Plato, St. Francis of Assisi, Johann Sebastian Bach, Sir Isaac Newton, are a few names which might be selected from many fields. All of us have had friends or relatives close to us who by the strength of their personality have left their influence upon us. Once we have known a powerful personality it is easy to believe that their magnetizing energy continues after the death of the physical body.

The Christian church has long believed that saints and loved ones continue to influence us after death. Seeking to guide us who are still on the earth-plane may they have caused guide-posts to be erected in our midst so that both the wise and simple will recall their message? Working through the minds of the architects of our most beautiful houses of worship they have placed the four symbols, man, lion, ox and eagle in hundreds of churches throughout Europe explaining the unique vision of each of the four gospels. The four evangelists, Matthew, Mark, Luke and John inspired the earth-plane creators of the cathedral of Chartres, a temple with a vibration of utmost purity, to place their signs in a prominent position over the main central door.

This holy edifice is dedicated to the lovely mother of Jesus, the Virgin Mary. Although Europe has many beautiful churches and cathedrals it is easy to accept the commonly-held judgment that this is the most perfect of the Gothic style. If one wanted to make sure that no one would miss the important message of the symbols what better way than to place them over the main entrance of this renowned sanctuary. Here we see the figure of Christ seated in glory, hand upraised in blessing. About him are four mysterious winged figures. To the eyes of tourists uneducated in the "lost language" they are meaningless. The tourist might assume them to be "decorations." If he is somewhat better educated he might know that these four winged creatures – a man, a lion, an ox and an eagle – represent the authors of the four gospels in the New Testament, Matthew, Mark, Luke and John. Nevertheless, our average tourist uninitiated in the deeper meanings of symbology is only scratching the surface of the total implications. Living in preliterate times, the people of the Middle Ages were steeped in the language of alchemy and astrology. To the worshipers of times long ago those four figures were radiant with living energy and articulating a wealth of meaning.

To the medieval worshiper it would be common knowledge that these four figures represented the four fixed points of the astrological compass. He would know that the four signs are the man, Aquarius; the lion, Leo; the ox, Taurus; and the eagle, Scorpio. He would be aware that they represent four distinct types of energy. All of the dynamic forces radiate from Christ who is the center, but each author picks up on just one vibration and describes the life of Jesus in those terms. For any worshiper about to enter the church on a sunny morning looking up at the symbols overhead the meanings were clear. Man is air, the lion is fire, the ox is the earth and the eagle water. From the tympanum above the lintel of the doorway he could see four unique styles of energy coming from Christ and going forth into the world. The man, air, represents intellectual vibrations, the thinking mind interrogating and explaining the universe. The lion represents power, fire, the driving forces which cause changes in the rest of the world. The ox depicts all things

32

earthy, the physical planet, growing things, the order and design which we unravel in the laws of chemistry and physics. The intuitive water sign is represented by the eagle, a bird flying high above the earth, looking down with spiritual eyes seeing the inner interpretation of all that exists.

Alert to the rich meaning of symbols those ancient ones knew that the four figures around Christ were far more than mere decorations. They knew that here was a spiritual compass with special meanings for certain individuals. It would be a rare person of the Middle Ages who did not know his horoscope. He surely knew his sun sign. He knew what it was to be a Capricorn or a Cancer and what would be the style of this kind of person. Then knowing his own style and capacities he knew which of the Christ energies would do him the greatest good. In the bewildering milieu of a lifetime of human relationships he had guideposts which would help him move most expeditiously to his greatest potential. If he were a Capricorn, an earth sign, he knew he would be most in harmony with the other earth signs, Taurus and Virgo. If he were an Aries he knew that his soul would be in trine, that is in most harmonious vibration, with the fiery Leos and Sagittarians. A Libran would look for the mental stimulation of an Aquarian or a Gemini. A Pisces would instinctively turn to the deep currents of the water signs, Cancer and Scorpio.

Our modern world is filled with millions of devout Bible students, yet among these multitudes few indeed recognize that each of the four symbols from the background of alchemy and astrology accurately describes the style of one of the four gospels. Once this understanding is made clear these four great books are instantly alive with new insights. Each one of the four gospels gives us a picture of Jesus Christ that is true and accurate. At the same time it is obvious that each representation is different, unique. That is to say each gospel author while doing his best to portray Jesus still comes up with a picture which is only a partial sketch. We would not say that any of the four is untrue, or one better than the others. It is only to say that each author described whatever he was capable of seeing. By putting all four together we come close to seeing the complete Christ.

We begin to see that a knowledge of the meaning and interpretation of the four symbols can be of extraordinary value to students of the life of Jesus. Especially is this true with regard to personal application of his teachings to our individual needs. All of us know that some people are better teachers for us than others. To the next person a different teacher may be the better instructor. Through the operation of the spiritual compass of the four symbols each person is able to quickly pick up that book of Christ's teachings which will be most relevant to his or her life style.

Historically the four gospels were created by characteristic individuals on behalf of special groups with both personal and national style in their manifestation. The first gospel, Matthew, signified by a man showing intellectual qualities, is written by a Jew for the Hebrew people. His major concern was to explain Jesus as the Jewish Messiah. He traces Jesus' genealogy to Abraham the founder of the Jewish race. Over and again he points out that Jesus did this or that "to fulfill" the ancient prophecies found in the old Jewish scriptures.

The gospel of Mark actually depicts the thoughts of Peter, the leading apostle, as recorded by his young friend, Mark. This fire sign gospel, appropriately under the symbol of Leo the lion, was especially relevant to the government, business and military personnel of the powerful Roman Empire. It shows no concern for fulfilling old Jewish prophecies or telling stories of Jesus' birth. Appealing to the vigorous leaders of the Empire Mark's gospel shows a man of power, a dynamic leader, who numbered among his abilities the power to drive out evil spirits and heal the sick in an instant.

34

It characteristically describes a high energy Jesus who "immediately" carries out this or that action.

Under the ox, an earth sign, we find Luke writing in "down to earth" style simple parables, colorful stories, which have been easily understood by peasant people all over the face of the earth. While Luke was a man of Greek culture and background nevertheless one has the feeling that he regards the whole earth as his home. The least nationalistic, it is the most universal of the gospels. Fittingly Luke traces Jesus' genealogy back to Adam, the founder of the human race.

John's gospel signified by the eagle contains the deepest spiritual insight of the four. Written by a "beloved disciple" who leaned upon the master's breast at the last supper this book is most helpful to those who have come alive through emotional attachment to others. With the penetrating eye of the eagle it sees through the mysteries of both this world and the next. In John's gospel the origin of the Christ power is seen not in Abraham, nor Adam, but in the logos, the word, at the beginning of time with God. The last of the four gospels, its insights are the most profound. It is the book for those who would go the furthest in seeking to know the meaning of the person Jesus Christ. Yet, strangely, this book can be understood by children, or anyone with a childlike, a simple faith.

Let us look again at the doorway of the beautiful Gothic cathedral, Chartres. We raise our eyes to the figure of Christ surrounded by the four beings. We no longer see "just decorations." With the insights of the "lost language," the symbolism of the Middle Ages, our souls begin to stir with the understanding which was theirs. Eyes opened with new comprehension we will see these symbols coming to us again and again in stained glass windows, paintings, tapestries and books. It begins to dawn on us that the worshipers in the days before general literacy might have had a Christian faith of deeper spiritual penetration, with wholeness of heart and mind, which we have been lacking in our "scientific" times. Relearning the lost language of symbolism is it possible that our lives can be renewed, gifted with certainty and power which has too often been in want?

A NEW SENSE OF DESTINY

Chapter 5

Intertwined with the Stars

Let us begin with the meaning of the first symbol, man. It explains the style of the first of the four gospels, Matthew. Apart from the style of the other three writings it lifts up the factor of human intelligence. Certainly one aspect of the person of Jesus Christ is an appeal to the human intellect. Matthew's gospel will be most appreciated by those persons who insist that life be reasonable; they want no part in the irrational. Matthew's gospel is for those persons who are constantly trying to see how all the bits and pieces of life fit together in some sort of meaningful pattern. This is precisely the kind of mind which was in Matthew. A follower of Jesus, he was a well educated Jew knowledgeable in the scriptures of his people. As he began to know Jesus, he was not only drawn to him as a vital person, a speaker and healer, Matthew was astounded to consider the possibility that this carpenter's son from Nazareth might be the long-awaited Messiah. As the life of Jesus was unfolding before his eyes he would sit back and meditate on the scriptures; soon he would see how the words of the prophets of old were being fulfilled in his sight.

Hearing that Jesus was born in Bethlehem he searched the scriptures and found the words in the prophet Micah, "And thou Bethlehem, in the land of Judah, art by no means least among the rulers of Judah; for from thee shall come a ruler who will govern my people Israel."[10] Later he recalled the words of Isaiah... "And he went and dwelt in a city called Nazareth, that what was spoken by the prophets might be fulfilled, 'He shall be called a Nazarene.' "[11] It is appropriate to the sign of the man, the intellectual factor, that Matthew recognized the life of Jesus fulfilling the prophetic utterances of Jews of centuries before.

If you are an air sign, Matthew's gospel should be the account of Christ's life which is for you most easily understood. If you are not an air sign, but are trying to deeply know some other person who is, then become acquainted with this book and its style. The "air signs" are people who desperately need to know that life makes sense. If they can read in the Bible that there are prophecies over hundreds of years indicating that God is working out a divine plan in the midst of what seem utterly random events their faith will be strengthened.

Those individuals whose primary attitude in approaching life is mental will appreciate the Sermon on the Mount which is found only in Matthew. We have a new science of the mind called psychology but none of its proponents have more succinctly stated the truths of the interplay of human personality than the prophet of Nazareth in this remarkable sermon. It is natural that it was Matthew with his "airy" mind who carefully recorded for us these thoughtful words. How many have carefully listened to thoughts such as these and changed the course of their lives? "Do not lay up for yourselves treasures on earth, where moth and rust consume and where thieves break in and steal, but lay up for yourselves treasures in heaven, where neither moth nor rust consumes and where thieves do not break in and steal; for where your treasure is, there will your heart be also."[12] How many millions of people have seen the wisdom of the Golden Rule and adopted it for their own behavior? "So whatever you wish that men would do to you, do so to them; for this is the law and the prophets."[13]

It is the nature of air sign minds to want to see all sides of a question and to deal with difficult points of justice. The story of the workers in the vineyard (Matthew 20:1-

16), deals with the complex problem of workers who have served on the job for various lengths of time. How can justice and mercy be equated under these circumstances? These are the kind of mental problems with which air sign people enjoy themselves. Would you understand them, get into their approach to living... read Matthew.

If you are an air sign, you have the potential for problem solving, for sitting on the judicial bench, for making new formulations of the understanding of human behavior in the sciences of psychology and sociology. On the other hand you would be wise to avoid job situations or social endeavors where one must carry on in spite of logic, when answers cannot be found. For you this would bring the ultimate in frustration. Look for channels where you can teach, learn, and put the pieces of life together in organized fashion.

Matthew's story of the marriage feast (22:1-14) has a special application to our times. A king invites the leading citizens, who are the logical guests, to a feast in honor of his son's wedding. These guests all claim to be too busy to come. So the king goes out among the ordinary folk in lesser walks of life to find a new group of guests who come and enjoy the feast. This suggests that in this new Aquarian age if the traditional structures of religion do not let the true energy of God flow through, then that power will find its way to the public through non-traditional channels.

It is Matthew's gospel which points out the interrelationship between the birth of Jesus and the positions of the planets. It is the magi, which some translate... the astrologers... who see the signs in the sky which draw them to Jerusalem and then to Bethlehem to witness the Messiah-child. There are overtones in this story to which we need to relate in a new way in the times in which we live. Twentieth century homo sapiens has, in a materialistic way, known more about the universe than any of our predecessors. At the same time we have been victimized by a limited interpretation of ourselves described as "behaviorism." In this school of thought for interpreting human existence we become what we are because of the attitudes toward us of our parents, family, and close associates. There is truth in this view but it is much too limited. It is Matthew's great insight to point out that the birth of Jesus was intertwined with the stars. He understood the ancient Hermetic phrase, "as above, so below." How our minds are stretched when we begin to think of a behaviorism which includes the universe to the farthest reaches of space!

Matthew's gospel is appropriately at the beginning of the New Testament where it serves as the bridge from the Old Testament to the New. Air sign people, especially Librans, are concerned to build bridges of understanding between groups of people who have not been able to get along with each other. Matthew set himself to the difficult task of explaining the Christian position to the traditional Jews. He sought to accomplish this by a carefully documented account showing that the man of Galilee was indeed the long-prophecied Messiah. Matthew's gospel is the best for those persons who are seeking to unravel the myriad puzzles of human existence through the mind of Christ voiced by the prophet of Nazareth.

A NEW SENSE OF DESTINY

Chapter 6

Restoring Our Inner Power

Looking at the four figures surrounding Christ in the tympanum above the central door of Chartres cathedral we can mentally turn the dial so that the cosmic energies flowing from Christ, the central figure, come through not on the vibration of the man, but of the lion. The source of the energy is still the Master, but the quality of the lion is much different from the man. Instead of following intellectual threads of thought, judicial niceties, or the linking of the prophecies, we come now to an appreciation of Jesus as a man of power. Mark's gospel is really the story of Jesus as seen through the eyes of the dynamic leader of the apostles, Peter. Mark was simply his secretary. Peter was a headstrong, forthright leader. For him life had to move. He would make more than his share of mistakes. To sit quietly and ponder the best possible way before acting would not be Peter's style.

As we tune in to the energies which flow through Mark and Peter we see how appropriate is the symbol of Leo, the lion. This book was composed by and for those persons whose life style is centered on the flow of power. Scholars point out that the thrust of Mark's gospel was to affect people who were of the Roman Empire. It is a dynamic story written to capture the attention of marching legions. It is for strong men skilled in use of sword and shield. It is a power book written for people accustomed to authority and the chain of command. These soldiers were unafraid of the attack of fierce lions. Like the king of beasts they were confident of their power to handle all situations. Also, the Roman world was an economic as well as a military empire. Its ships with daring sailors, and fearless merchants traveled to the far borders and brought rare goods back to Rome. The empire's businessmen much like leaders of industry today honored those who "got things done."

Mark's gospel is the briefest of the four. The Romans had no interest in the old Jewish prophecies of a Messiah as described in Matthew. Nor would they take precious time to listen to the well-turned parables in Luke. Instead, in as few words as possible, Peter presents Jesus as an authority figure, who speaks with a dynamic energy to which people instantly respond.

The key word in this book is "immediately." Over and again this word is used to describe his ministry. He calls the disciples by the seashore and they "immediately" drop their nets and follow him. A leper asks to be cleansed and through the healing power in Christ "immediately" the leprosy leaves him. He "sternly" charges those who are healed to say nothing. The onlookers are "astonished" at the power of his healing and his words. Seeing the paralytic "immediately" walk "they were all amazed and glorified God saying, 'We never saw anything like this!' "

After the collapse of the Roman world during the Dark Ages there was little of law and order, courts and the niceties of civilization. Rule was established by bands of armed men with the keenness of their swords. The power and authority of the Jesus seen through Mark's gospel would get their attention. The kings on thrones and their armored knights would listen to a man whose energies could cause others to do his will, heal the sick and raise the dead. All toilers who involve the total intensity of their being, muscles, heart and emotions and demand the same of fellow workers will value this Jesus. Those of today, who know that it is the dynamic of personality which makes the business world move, appreciate this Jesus.

Mark's Leo-Christ can enrich two quite opposite types of personality. First, there are those extroverts who feel themselves most alive when energy is freely flowing through their personality to others. When they are in this power stream they are happy and enjoy their lives. They will appreciate Mark's Christ. At the opposite extreme there are those low-energy types... who need a renewal of vitality. Seeing the Jesus described by Mark their inner nature responds and is strengthened into new life and activity. Apathetic persons who are sensitive to music would do well to listen to works such as the Mars section from Gustave Holsts's, THE PLANETS. In this segment the composer has captured the essence of driving energy. It would be difficult to listen to music like this and remain languid.

Perhaps we are at a point in life where we are wondering whether or not we should accept a new major challenge. If so, we do well to read Mark, Peter's gospel, and feel the energy of Leo, the lion, pouring through us. If timidity is our problem, let us place pictures of lions on our walls, or a carved figure of the king of beasts on our desk. Low energy, fears, cowardice cannot co-exist with the lion-like temperament.

If your sun is in one of the fire signs – Aries, Leo, or Sagittarius, or if you have several planets in fire signs then you are one of those persons who love to be in the flow of powerful energies. For your life to be satisfying you must share in some sort of group life where you are a part of the electricity which is getting things accomplished. You thrive in a chain of command where important responsibilities are being carried out. Read Mark's gospel where you will see a Christ of extraordinary power, one whose exciting energies "immediately" changed the lives of those about him from drabness to joy, from sickness to health, from hopelessness to victory. For people of high energy style who have erroneously dismissed Jesus as "meek and mild," Mark's gospel is an eye-opener. Here they will see a Jesus who heals the sick and raises the dead, and even commands the elements stilling a storm on the lake. They will read about a person with such extraordinary control of the material plane of existence that he is able to walk on water. They will see a person who is such a perfect channel for spiritual energies that in the transfiguration experience on the mountaintop his body will glow with an unearthly light.

High energy, fire sign people, will delight in such a Jesus. Because he is of their style, they will quickly and deeply empathize with this aspect of his personality. Though he may be a thousand times more energized than their own lives nevertheless they will recognize that they are of the same fiery substance, and they will readily follow him into greater personal fulfillment.

While I have no figures to prove it, I suspect that the majority of the world's population has more timidity than lion-like courage. We tend to be frightened by trials of living. While the struggles and battles of the earth rage around us we would prefer to hide in some quiet, peaceful corner. At worst we become psychological mummies as described by Algernon Charles Swinburne.

"The burden of long living. Thou shalt fear
Waking, and sleeping mourn upon thy bed;
And say at night 'Would God the day were here,'
And say at dawn, "Would God the day were dead'." [14]

If such a description fits our character for even part of our conscious lives we need to steep ourselves in the dynamic Christ portrayed in Mark's gospel. The worshipers in the churches and cathedrals in times prior to Herr Gutenberg and the printing press probably were more effective than we are today in turning frightened sheep into roaring lions. Not being numbed by the reading of thousands of pages in books and magazines as we are, those illiterates of earlier times had a more vital, a more total relationship, to the stories of the Bible. They saw the stories being enacted before their eyes in statuary, stained glass, and paintings. Seeing, rather than reading about the heroic deeds of Bible times, their brain waves would have registered a greater amplitude and power. Deeply involved in heart and emotions, there would have been a greater likelihood of the creation of lion-like personalities.

Let us go into a 12th century cathedral and imagine a little knot of peasants gathered around a bas-relief of Jesus stilling the tempest. We can hear them talking together in whispers about the story. They could imagine themselves in fright as the waves crashed against the side of the boat. They feel the wind tipping the vessel ever more dangerously on its side. More and more the waves are spilling into the hull and there is fear that the boat might go down with all lives lost. Unbelievably, the Master's faith is so great that he lies sleeping in the storm-tossed ship. Finally the disciples' fear overcomes their awe of Jesus and they wake him... "Master... we are perishing." He instantly sees their distress and speaks to the sea... "Peace! Be still!" The wind ceases and there is a great calm. The peasants can imagine themselves among the disciples muttering, "Who then is this, that even wind and sea obey him?"[15]

Those worshipers of old were so involved, by learning through a variety of the visual arts, that they received a depth of meaning which you and I of the present day booklearning generation rarely know. Ignatius of Loyola, 1491-1556, founder of the Jesuits, working in the days when books were only beginning to become common property, was aware of the need for the total involvement of the individual for a Bible story to have its deepest meaning. In his highly successful devotional exercises he would encourage his monks to recreate with all of their senses what it would be like to be present at some moment in the life of Christ. If it were the night of Jesus' betrayal by Judas in the garden of

A NEW SENSE OF DESTINY

Gethsemane on the Mount of Olives Ignatius would have them imagine the smell of the olive trees, the feel of the earth under foot, the sound of the marching soldiers with clashing steel as they come to take Jesus. They would see the flames of the torches casting shadows among the trees. Let them taste the salt of the perspiration brought on by the tension of the disciples and the heat of the night. Let them listen to the calls of the night birds. And then in the midst of all this seeing and feeling sense how the disciples are cut to the heart as their leader is led away under armed guard. This is how Bible stories truly come alive.

Isn't it obvious to most of us that we have fallen far short of our potential week after week because we were in want of courage? It's not a new problem. This is the heart-theme of Hamlet in Shakespeare's play who has him speaking for so many of us as he says, "The native hue of resolution is sicklied o'er with the pale cast of thought, and enterprizes of great pitch and moment with this regard their currents turn awry, and lose the name of action."[16] If our lives slip into a thin soup of rationality with no heart, soul, or emotion we will never accomplish anything of consequence. If we must honestly confess that too often we have hemmed and hawed while braver souls moved on, then let the Leo-Christ show us the way.

Perhaps someday acid rain will extinguish the life in our lakes and our forests will die, but there is another danger to mankind not often acknowledged. Could it simply be that our brains become too tired and frazzled by tons and tons of often meaningless paper work. Perhaps the fire of living will die, smothered by too many reports which in time wind up gathering dust in some government warehouse. Yes, we need to fear the danger of the disposal of atomic waste, but should we not also be frightened for the loss of fiery desire to live to the fullness of what it means to be human. T. S. Eliot stated succinctly,

"We are the hollow men
We are the stuffed men
Leaning together
Headpiece filled with straw. Alas!
Our dried voices, when
We whisper together
Are quiet and meaningless
As wind in dry grass
Or rats' feet over broken glass
In our dry cellar.
This is the way the world ends
Not with a bang but a whimper." [17]

But is must not be that way. I believe that God has placed a divine spark in the hearts of human beings. When this little spark is introduced to the presence of the power in the Leo-Christ it surges into a beautiful, living flame. This energy, the fire in the human breast, is of more significance, more consequence, than atomic power. When civilizations seem to be going into their last days, when morality is no more than dry rot, when vision is lost and hope cannot be found, God sends us new prophets, fearless martyrs to whom righteousness and justice mean more than life itself. A new flame of the spirit arises in the hearts of humanity. May the awesome power in Christ, seen through the eyes of Peter and his author Mark, keep us ever alive, ready to do and dare.

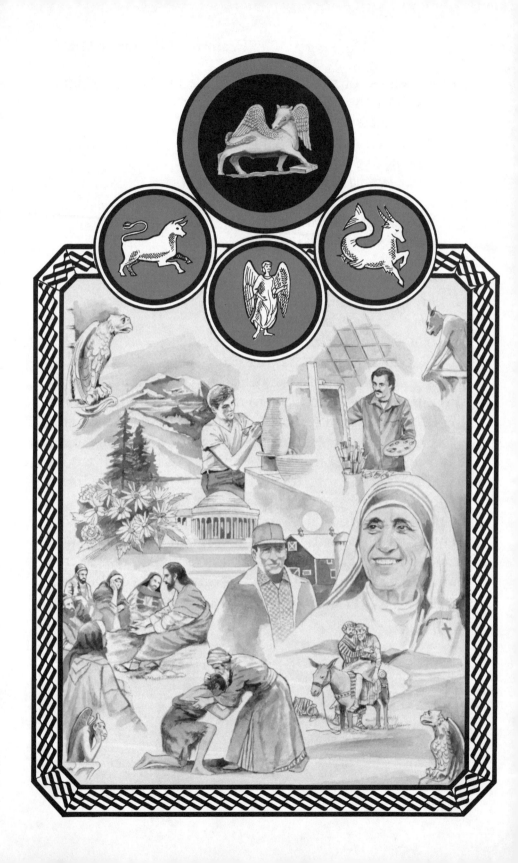

A NEW SENSE OF DESTINY

Chapter 7

Down to Earth Practicality

Once more we look at the four symbols around Jesus as seen over the central entrance of Chartres cathedral or similar prominent places in other churches. This time we consider the cosmic energies flowing in from the Universal Creator through Christ the mediator coming to us through the ox. In astrological symbolism this figure represents Taurus, the bull, and brings us vibrations relevant for earth sign people. These denizens of the soil are realistic, literally "down-to-earth" folks. As Taureans, they are sensitive to colors, to touch and to taste. They appreciate their living in this world with the glories of the sunset and the radiant beauty of many-hued flowers. As Taureans they are willing to be prodigious workers as farmers in the fields or with any tasks that have them grappling daily with the physical necessities of life. They are always seeking to add a touch of beauty to the daily round, such as, at the end of each row in the vineyard planting a graceful flower.

If they are Virgos they will want to classify and place in practical structure the units of life about them. Neatness... careful organization... are their watchwords. Should they be Capricorns they will take the industry of the Taurean, the systematization of the Virgo, and working to satisfy practical human needs, will see their efforts crowned with success. Capricorns want "to put it all together" and will see that their earth energies are not wasted, but add up to positive contributions in which the participants attain a recognized achievement. Working long and hard in the material world they achieve useful results. By the labor of the hands of the "earth" people our planet becomes more beautiful and fruitful.

A NEW SENSE OF DESTINY

The Gospel of Luke is a book which practical persons above all can understand. In contrast to Matthew's gospel written with an intellectual approach having special significance concerning prophecies for the Jewish nation, and Mark's gospel recorded for the Roman world and its dynamic military and commerical leaders, Luke's gospel is for all mankind. Here the genealogy of Jesus is traced not just to Abraham, the founder of the Jewish nation, but rather to Adam, the father of the entire human race. Less concerned for fulfilling the ancient prophecies of Israel, Luke is more interested in portraying a Jesus who is one with all humanity. Luke sees a Christ who is the supreme story-teller, whose parables deal with life-situations which occur again and again in many forms throughout the world. His stories of the Good Samaritan, the Rich Fool, the Prodigal Son, and the Rich Man and Lazarus have been written indelibly into the hearts of human beings of all races and creeds.

Who are the people who need to absorb the earth energies of Christ? As I have indicated, any persons who are of the astrological earth signs will feel most at home in this gospel, but I would quickly add another major group. These are the individuals who somehow feel unimportant in their position in the social order. Do you feel lost in the shuffle because you are poor and hungry, because you are of a minority race or religion, because you are a woman, or a child, too young, or too old? Then this book is for you. Luke vividly tells the story of Jesus' birth in Bethlehem. Here is a family for whom there is no room in the inn, but must be put out in the barn with the animals, and this at the crucial moment when a birth is imminent. How all the poor, the little people in the Third World countries, can empathize with a child born in such humble circumstances!

How often do we feel that we are slighted because we don't belong to the right group. We are turned down for

54

a job, salespeople turn away from us, or we are refused entrance into a certain social group or club. If our hearts have been wounded by the slights of prejudice, then how penetrating is the story of the Good Samaritan. The "in group" individuals who should have been most helpful simply passed by the man who had been wounded and robbed. Help came from a member of a despised group, the Samaritans, who were outside the orthodox Jewish faith. In that unforgettable story Jesus is telling us that the true love of God is expressed by individuals who let their good acts transcend national and religious barriers.

Who else needs to read this earth energy book? How about the person prosperous in material goods? Luke tells the story of the rich man who hoped to improve his happiness by amassing more and more grain and goods, building ever larger barns in which to store them. This proves foolishness, for his life is to end that very night. It is much more important to build up treasure toward God through acts of love and mercy.

Anyone caught up in the distress of interpersonal relationship... fathers and sons... mothers and daughters... brothers and sisters... cannot help but respond to the insights offered through the story of the Prodigal Son. How many of us, having lost ourselves in dissolute living, one day come to our senses and return to our father seeking forgiveness? Our heart goes out to the father who having forgiven the younger son, must still deal with the jealousy of the older son. True to life stories like this can help us attain peace and harmony in our personal and international families.

Earth people are appealed to through their senses. Luke's gospel is filled with adjectives from a baby wrapped in "swaddling clothes," to "fresh wineskins" for new wine, to a woman bringing an "alabaster" flask of ointment, or Jesus in agony in Gethsemane with "sweat like great drops of blood falling down upon the ground." Luke appeals to our senses using color and texture describing a rich man "clothed in purple and fine linen." This book appeals to the sense of hearing. It is filled with the sounds of the day and night from heavenly choirs heralding the cry of a newborn child... to the cries of the sick for healing... the glad shouts of the hungry who have been fed... the murmuring of evil ones who would destroy Jesus... the prophecied signal of a cock crow... the startled in-breathing by those who first see the resurrected Lord... the excited voices of two men on the road to Emmaus as they tried to retell their experience, "Did not our hearts burn within us while he talked to us on the road?"[18]

For people of the earth signs it is helpful to know that they will be most fulfilled when their energies are expressed through things of this world. They are the farmers, the builders, the artisans, the weavers and dyers making clothes of many colors. They love flowers and gardening, and are sensitive to shadows and light. If you are an earth person you will find your greatest happiness in contributing to the ongoing practical business of the world. It will be most meaningful if the work can be more than mere routine... that is, if it will give you an opportunity to express beauty, color, design, through creative artistry.

It will be earth sign people who best understand Jesus' saying, "Blessed are the meek for they shall inherit the earth."[19] Earth folks humbly bend their bodies as they plant the seed... hoe the weeds... fight crop predators... and harvest, not on the day which suits one's fancy, but on that right day when the crops are perfectly matured. The great Dutch artist, Rembrandt, had the knack of seeing the greatness of God in the faces and figures of all the little people... the everyday toilers. His illustrations of the Bible stories show a loving concern for the simple people of the land. With his marvelous use of light he suggested the radiance of

God's glory in the midst of the common-place. A master-piece is his painting of Christ at Emmaus showing two men who suddenly recognized the glorious light of the universe shining through the stranger who had walked and talked with them.

How about the people for whom the earth expression is not their style? If the man-intellect, lion-energy, or eagle-spirit typifies your life-style what does earth sign living mean to you? We know that electrical appliances do not work safely unless they are grounded. In the same way those other three energies may not be safe unless they are rooted in common, every-day life experiences. If we are not of the earth style... it would be wise to have some for our co-workers... in order that our planning and energies be rooted in reality. In our zeal to be thinkers and doers, and to give spiritual life, may we never get out of touch with the great host of common humanity in the midst of daily exigencies. Luke's gospel sees the light of Christ being shed forth to all members of the human race... the children of Adam. Before this interpretation of the Master all national and racial barriers fall. The sign of the ox symbolizing everything of the earth is a necessary quadrant without which we cannot find wholeness within ourselves or with God's children of every race and tongue.

A NEW SENSE OF DESTINY

Chapter 8

Seeing the Cosmic in Every Day

When first touring the cathedrals of Europe I failed to have any understanding of the four figures around Christ thinking of them as mere decorations. Had some artist let his imagination run on with no special meaning? One reason why it was a long time before the four symbols gained meaning for me was the problem of the significance of the eagle. It had not taken a long time for me to become aware that the four signs were to be interpreted as the four evangelists, the authors of the four gospels... that was reasonably clear. In many illuminated manuscripts of these books one finds the signs, Matthew – the man, Mark – the lion, Luke – the ox, and John – the eagle. But to think of the four as representing a deeper mystical level was hidden from me because one sign, the eagle, is not commonly known as an astrological symbol in modern studies. If the first three signs fitted the picture of air, fire, and earth, the fourth did not. Therefore, any interpretation of the gospels as relating to the four states of being described in the combined symbolism of alchemy and astrology was denied me.

The key which unlocked this understanding was given to me by an astrological friend who is a Scorpio. One day she happened to say to me, "I don't like to think of myself as a scorpion. Do you know that Scorpio is really a dual sign?... its other symbol is the eagle. I like to fly as an eagle." With these words I suddenly had the key; another level of interpretation of the four beasts was now clear. The four gospels are not simply identified as to their authorship by the names Matthew, Mark, Luke and John; indeed, we can go more broadly to the ancient symbols of alchemy, air, fire, earth and water. It now dawned on me that the ancients were clearly seeing four distinct styles, four separate vibrations expressed through these books. As we read and reread them it gradually becomes clear that somehow the writing of each of these books was chiseled in one of the four definitive styles of alchemy; a unique expression of the power of the Creator of the cosmos channeled through Jesus of Nazareth subject to the manner of perception of each gospel author. In Christ the light of all four signs is shining at once, but even as the rainbow breaks white light down into the various glowing hues, so each of the four gospel writers captured one quadrant of that light in a distinctive fashion.

To look directly into the sun on a clear day is too much for the human eye. To look straight into the eyes of Christ, or to follow perfectly in his footsteps, is more than most of us can accomplish. We can better understand sunlight as we see its glorious power reflected on the colors of autumn leaves, dancing across the waves of a sea at early evening, or reflected on the faces of family and friends whom we love. In the same way the light of God in Christ reflected through the vision of each of the gospel writers gives us pictures on which we can linger as we grow in understanding.

John's gospel is for the water signs, Cancer, Scorpio, Pisces people, intuitive, emotionally sensitive. Its style is fitting for the beloved young disciple who sat closest to Jesus at the Last Supper. Even the most casual reader will note that the account by John is different from the other three gospels. It builds its unique characteristic not only by the feel of its presentation, but also by major changes in the amount of words used to describe certain events in the life of Jesus. For example, the Last Supper receives only a few lines in the first three accounts, but is stretched in full detail through five chapters as recorded in John. Matthew, Mark, and Luke stroll through the scenery and events surrounding the life of Jesus each seeing in their own way, but following the same general plan. In quite different fashion John's gospel is the eagle's flight over the scene. Looking from far above it is a penetrating spiritual insight into Christ and his relationships with those about him. The purpose of the Gospel of John is not simply to tell the story of the life of Jesus; its purpose is to explain the profound inner significance of the events.

For example, John's gospel is not concerned to link the birth of Jesus with the Jews through Abraham, as Matthew noted; nor is it concerned to trace the genealogy of Jesus back to Adam, the founder of the human race as noted by Luke. John's gospel speaks with deeper insight. He perceives Christ as the divine creative energy from the beginning of time. "In the beginning was the Word, and the Word was with God, and the Word was God. He was in the beginning with God; all things were made through him, and without him was not anything made that was made."[20]

Those who are familiar with the thinking of the great priest-paleontologist, Pierre Teilhard de Chardin, find a responsive chord. Looking across the billions of years of the planet's history Teilhard recognized what he calls "radial energy" which he believed was a "something within" which is ever striving to build more complex forms. It was apparent to him that the history of the universe is not simply the dispersing and dying of great heat, a process called entropy. Instead he could see a mysterious "other" which he named "radial energy" always leading to higher forms, and eventually higher and higher consciousness. He noted that this force rises from mineral to plant to animal and to the remarkable human brain. As a scientist digging in the bones of past ages he verified the words of the Persian poet, Jalaluddin Rumi, who wrote in the 13th century...

61

"I died as a mineral and became a plant,
I died as a plant and rose to animal,
I died as animal and I was Man.
Why should I fear? When was I less by dying?
Yet once more I shall die as Man, to soar
With angels blest...."[21]

John's gospel sees that divine creative energy from the beginning of time personified for our understanding in the Nazarene. This thought is expressed in similar terms in such expressions as, "I am the bread of life."[22] "He who eats my flesh and drinks my blood abides in me, and I in him."[23] Through the incarnation of the Christ we were all given new hope of what our lives might become. His coming was for the raising of consciousness of all humanity. "The true light that enlightens every man was coming into the world."[24] "In him was life, and the life was the light of man."[25]

Who are the people who have the greatest natural rapport with this water sign book? They are the Cancers, whose approach to life is primarily through emotions and feelings. Or the Scorpios, who beam into life through the intensity of their desires. Or the Pisceans, whose empathy with the world comes through their beliefs, convictions, not so much of the mind as of the heart. Perhaps your sun sign is not in water, but if your moon or Jupiter, or a cluster of planets, is in one of these three water signs, then John's gospel, the spiritual interpretation of the Christ is for you. Here is where you will find your soul best nourished... most at home.

John's gospel is filled with deep, emotional love. From the story of the raising of Lazarus we receive a characterization of the Master in the unique style of John and the water signs. "Then Mary, when she came where Jesus was and saw him, fell at his feet saying to him, 'Lord, if you had been here, my brother would not have died.' When Jesus saw her weeping, and the Jews who came with her also weeping, he was deeply moved in spirit and troubled; and he said, 'Where have you laid him?' They said to him, 'Lord, come and see.' Jesus wept."[26] The Master empathized with those who cared... nor would he disdain tears for himself.

It is not significant that we simply take part in reading a book filled with emotions... it is important that we learn to not be abused by our feelings, but to direct them... ride them to the best possible outcome. It is good to have sympathy, caring in our hearts, and then ride those emotional energies into practical acts on behalf of those in need. Think of the picture of the disciple John leaning close to the Master at the table of the Last Supper hearing him say... "Truly, truly, I say to you, he who believes in me will also do the works that I do; and greater works than these will he do..."[27] We should see ourselves as branches on the vine that is Christ. When the emotional energy of holiness coming from him moves through our lives... then are we most exalted... most useful to others... most self-fulfilled.

There is also value in John's gospel for those persons who have little or no water signs in their charts. If you are mostly air, fire, or earth you may have trouble relating emotionally to the water sign folks. To air signs those water people seem to rely too much on instinct... hunches. To fire people the water signs lack drive... they seem to be leaners... too gushy... cry babies. To earth folks the water signs lack down to earth practicality. They may have lots of concern and love... but what good is that without some visible expression. Nevertheless, in the long run we are all striving to become whole persons. In the every day rough and tumble of life where we are constantly living with all sorts of people, John's gospel will help us to understand those persons who live primarily in their emotions, desires, and beliefs. Let the non-water signs get an education here.

A NEW SENSE OF DESTINY

For those who are water signs, naturally at home in this gospel, and for those to whom such a life style is something in which they need education, there is deep learning here to be found. As highly educated citizens working with books, newspapers, and magazines it is easy to be so mentally oriented we have not let the emotional side of our lives have its fair place. This is especially true for men. As people with a great deal of drive for success in practical, down to earth affairs, we have not often chosen the way of meditation... seeking to build the spiritual. We need to live more on the right side of the brain in the slower and deeper levels of alpha and theta consciousness. John's gospel is for those who seek to develop the mystical ranges of being. For twentieth century civilized humanity this has not been our style... the truth is we have so missed this side of the expression of our being that it now demands to be reborn.

John's gospel is appropriately the last of the four. Having read the story of Jesus in three different ways now we are seeking to penetrate to its deepest meanings. If Matthew, Mark, and Luke tell us how to live in this world in a present lifetime, John's gospel does this, but also tells us of a world beyond. Matthew in the Sermon on the Mount gives a supreme interpretation of the psychological nuances of daily existence. Mark's gospel sees the release of divine energies through the Christ and his disciples into every situation where there is a problem which needs action and healing... and there can be no delay. Luke's gospel reminds us of the needs of all people whatever their race or religion.

John's gospel more deeply interprets for us what has been described in the previous three books. He sees the life of Jesus Christ as the interpenetration of two worlds. The mind of God from higher planes is being made known to us through Jesus in everyday experiences we can all understand. "About the middle of the feast Jesus went up into the temple and taught. The Jews marveled at it, saying, 'How is it that this man has learning, when he has never studied?' So Jesus answered them, 'My teaching is not mine, but his who sent me; if any man's will is to do his will, he shall know whether the teaching is from God or whether I am speaking on my own authority.'"[28]

John's gospel coming to us on the profound empathy vibrations of the water signs, explains that the mind of God is being made known in our midst through the person of Jesus the Christ. It is a fitting climax to the four gospels. This spiritual interpretation is best understood after we have first assimilated the events in the life of Jesus, and the stories which he told, as described in the earlier narratives. The fourth gospel is that place where we begin to feel ourselves at home in God's universe as we become whole persons.

As John's story of Jesus grips us we come together mind and heart, intellect and emotions, left and right brain. The divine and the mundane, the sacred and the secular, are no longer separate categories of being. The holy is not something done one day, or one hour of the week, as separate from the rest of our doing and being. We appreciate the words of Minot J. Savage...

"Men look for God and fancy him concealed;
But in earth's common things he stands revealed
While grass and flowers and stars spell out his name."[29]

Schizophrenia is the characteristic disease of Western civilization. It is an illness which has let mind and heart think they could exist separately. This is utterly wrong. It is a disease which has falsely assumed that we could take an objective stance somehow outside the world in which we exist... which simple facts prove absurd. Pioneers in medical and mental therapies are beginning to recognize the necessity of reaching the entire person if any healing is going to last. Chemotherapy and x-ray may destroy cancer cells, but if a person is in total despair the body's natural immune reactions will be turned off and there will be no long term healing.

A NEW SENSE OF DESTINY

John's gospel is from the eye of the soaring eagle, whose gaze penetrates to the smallest blade of grass on the terrain. It is that gospel which is able to bring healing to the whole person. Here mind and heart can become one. In these pages one finds spirit interfused with the material world. Here each human being in the midst of pressures of a multitude of daily events still finds himself in tune, in harmony with, the eternal. Our schizophrenia, split personality, is gone. We are truly at one in God.

When Jesus knew that he had come to his last opportunity to talk with his disciples freely and at length... the occasion was the Last Supper in the upper room in Jerusalem... he closed the evening with a great prayer for unity. This prayer has been most commonly interpreted as a prayer that his disciples stay together to work as a unified body. This text has been much used by those Christian leaders who have been trying in recent years to build world-wide Christian unity... the ecumenical movement. When the words were first given voice Jesus probably felt if each disciple went apart from the others, even though each individual might be a good person, still the moving power of the early church would have been destroyed by too much fragmentation... too much individuality. However, as we turn our thought to again study Jesus' closing prayer I think it is possible we can read into these words another interpretation. It is an exposition which can bring healing of the schizophrenia of modern Western humanity. Let us recall the scene.

In a dark room, dimly lit by a few oil lamps, the disciples have finished their meal, Jesus has spoken, and now he is in prayer. Though there is the sound of passersby outside, within the room all is intense concentration on the Master as he prays... "I do not pray for these only, but also for those who are to believe in me through their word, that they may all be one; even as thou, Father, art in me, and I in thee, that they also may be in us, so that the world may believe that thou has sent me."[30]

In daily parlance we say of someone we admire, "He's got it all together." By this we don't mean to say that this person has brought together a great sum of worldly possessions. Rather we are saying that this person on a deep level has quit fighting with himself... he has achieved unity within his own being. Multitudes in our times are troubled with trying to go too many ways at once. Students of the mind have invented a new word to describe this unhappy state. They say such a person has dysponesis... literally a scattering of energies... the opposite of a unified being who "has got it all together."

Can we say that in this great prayer Jesus is not only praying for his individual disciples to work as a team, but also that each disciple be a whole person... deeply unified in body, mind, and spirit? "That they may be one even as we are one."[31] We want to be people who've "got it all together." We want to stop this everlasting quarrel within ourselves which for too many people is never solved... only subdued by a host of tranquilizing drugs.

John's gospel more than the other three lets us see ourselves as whole persons. That is, we are not just physical bodies born of the cells of our parents; in truth, we are in the deepest essence spiritual beings temporarily encased in bodies of human flesh. In the third chapter of John's gospel Jesus in discourse with a ruler of the Jews, Nicodemus, says... "that which is born of the flesh is flesh, and that which is born of the Spirit is spirit."[32] There is another plane of existence interpenetrating and directing the physical. John's gospel describes these intermingling worlds.

A NEW SENSE OF DESTINY

Jesus in his prayer at the Last Supper is sensing that unity which is to be found when we recognize that we are of God, in God... that in no way can we exist apart from the Creator. When our mental and physical activities are directed by God we are at one within.... we are whole persons... happy... healed. "The glory which thou has given me I have given to them, that they may be one even as we are one, I in them and thou in me, that they may become perfectly one..."[33] This is the glorious affirmation of the intention of our being as divine spirits created by the hand of God as seen through the Gospel of John.

A NEW SENSE OF DESTINY

Chapter 9

A Wider View

Up to this point the main focus of our study has been on the symbolism found in the beautiful churches of Europe which were planned and constructed during the 10th through the 13th centuries. While the four styles of energies of God were exquisitely manifest in the four gospels written soon after the time of Jesus, and captured for the Christian congregations of the Middle Ages in the art of the cathedrals, in fact this division of four major modes of expression is universal in time and place.

There are suggestions of the four-fold powers in prehistoric stone age cultures. Without written records we cannot be certain of the interpretation. Sumer in southern Iraq may rightfully claim to be the oldest known civilization. In the 4th and 3rd milleniums B.C. it had picto-graphic and cuneiform writing with well developed literature. In Sumerian art we find the roots of the fourfold styles with pictures composed of a lion, an eagle and a peacock mounted on the back of an ox.

Turning to the Far East "According to Chocod, the equivalent Chinese animals afford the following correspondences: the dragon corresponding to the lion, the unicorn to the bull, the turtle to Man, the phoenix to the eagle."[34] Nevertheless, "It is to the Christian tetramorphs, with their synthesis of the four symbols of the Evangelists, that we are bound to look for the purest and truest expression of this ancient and universal idea."[35]

While roots of the four energy styles can be found in Sumer, Egypt and throughout the Middle East one linkage deserves special recognition. The symbols of Judaism and

Christianity are deeply interwoven. It was in celebrating the Passover that Jesus instituted the Last Supper. With his crucifixion his followers would think of him as the sacrificial lamb of ancient Jewish rites. To write of the impact of the symbols of the four evangelists while neglecting their evidence in the Old Testament would be false to the full story of the development of these historical religions.

Almost 600 years before the coming of Jesus of Nazareth the Jewish people were given ecstatic visions of a prophet named Ezekiel. At that point in its history the Hebrew nation had been overcome by military might and many of its people, especially leading citizens, had been taken captive into Babylonia. While in prison Ezekiel, the priest, the son of Buzi, was given by the spirit of God this remarkable vision.

"As I looked, behold, a stormy wind came out of the north, and a great cloud, with brightness round about it, and fire flashing forth continually, and in the midst of the fire, as it were gleaming bronze. And from the midst of it came the likeness of four living creatures. And this was their appearance; they had the form of men, but each had four faces, and each of them had four wings. Their legs were straight, and the soles of their feet were like the sole of a calf's foot; and they sparkled like burnished bronze. Under their wings on their four sides they had human hands. And the four had their faces and their wings thus; their wings touched one another; they went every one, straight forward without turning as they went. As for the likeness of their faces, each had the face of a *man* in front, the four had the face of a *lion* on the right side, the four had the face of an *ox* on the left side, and the four had the face of an *eagle* at the back."[36] It is now obvious that the symbols used in identifying the four evangelists did not have their beginning with the writing of the four gospels.

Let's set the stage for the time of Ezekiel's vision. The Hebrew people defeated in battle, suffering as slaves in Babylon, were dreaming, hoping, of some day being returned in independence to their homeland. It was Ezekiel's vision that indeed there would be a restoration of their people to Israel. His vision was accurate for it is historically true that some years later the Jewish people were set free and did return to their former country. While that prediction for a short span of time proved true we must attempt to try to deal with the possibility that the same vision was incorporating events which would be manifest centuries later in the four gospels of Jesus Christ. To present day scientific minds this sounds like foolish double-talk. Either Ezekiel was describing an event to be immediately fulfilled, or miracle of miracles, he was somehow foreseeing a happening which would not occur for hundreds of years. To Western minds schooled in the precision of Aristotle it would be unthinkable to accept his vision as describing both circumstances. Here is where we must learn one of the great lessons of the use of symbolism.

Can we imagine how difficult it will be in the year 4,000 A.D. to understand our ways of life? Will those dwellers in future centuries surmise that we worshiped a small, black mouse whose name was Mickey, not realizing the mouse was a cartoon figure for children? Present day archaeologists probing the pyramids and tombs of ancient Egypt would be fortunate to half describe the actual style of life of those days. Nevertheless, I believe it is worth our time to attempt to understand the imagery and prophecy in the Bible.

Basically we must recognize that in the Near East the use of symbols and images in speaking and writing was then far more open and flexible and remains so today. In the use of Near Eastern language it is acceptable that there can be several different levels of perception at the same time.

A NEW SENSE OF DESTINY

The mystical Sufis, for example, point out that a peach may be admired simply for the beauty of its color... the pink and orange of the ripening fruit. Or it can be appreciated for its lovely aroma. On another level it can be eaten and enjoyed for the value of its nutrition to the body. Some enjoy cracking the delicious kernel in the center of the fruit. Where fuel is scarce these shells can be be collected and burned for cooking. In the time and culture of the writing of the Bible in just the same way there could be meanings on different levels. We are missing highs and lows, light and shade, various hues, if we fail to appreciate the breadth of interpretations of symbolic language.

Let's look at a particular story. From the second chapter of Matthew's gospel we pick up the narrative after the birth of Jesus. In a dream an angel appears to Joseph and warns him to flee with Mary and the infant because Herod the king is coming to destroy this person who might someday be a rival. Accepting the guidance of the dream Joseph, Mary with the baby, rise at night and flee safely into Egypt. Matthew is well acquainted with the ancient Jewish scriptures and after researching them declares, "This was to fulfill what the Lord had spoken by the prophet, 'Out of Egypt have I called my son.'"[37]

In fact, this is a reference to a prophecy given by Hosea about 700 years before Christ which in its context obviously points to an event many years prior when Moses led the Israelites out of slavery in Egypt. To Western minds schooled in modern science these vague symbols with overlapping meanings present immense difficulties. We are accustomed to thinking that something must be specific, it is either this, or it is that. To the Oriental mind this was no problem. They could see that the message was capable of several interpretations. Matthew would not be disturbed that Hosea might be referring at the same time to two different events... one hundreds of years before... the other hundreds of years later. In truth, to his type of mind, there would be a special appeal in the rhythmic repetition of the events of life at various times and places.

In the light of the open use of imagery, having no problem with the repetition of symbols in different settings, how may we then describe the relationship between Ezekiel's vision and the writing style of the four gospels? Shortly after 600 B.C. the prophet Ezekiel had a vision of four living creatures appearing out of a stormy wind from the north. On each one of the beings there was the face of a man, a lion, an ox, and an eagle. What was the vision saying to the Jews of that time? Helpless in captivity it gave them hope that God would be coming to their rescue. Precisely how this would happen they did not know, but the vision indicated that four different styles of power were at work on behalf of their cause. In later centuries with the writing of the four gospels further interpretation of these styles of energies would become clear. Over hundreds of years those who understood symbolic language could quickly capture the style and feel of Matthew as air, Mark... fire, Luke... earth, and John as water.

Present day scholarship may be precise, but unfortunately fails to give the fullness of dimension which the ancients understood in the four symbols. The limited scope of many current scholarly commentaries on the four figures can be shown by descriptions such as these. [Matthew is represented by a man because this gospel begins with a listing of the ancestors of Jesus.] [Mark's figure is the lion because the book opens with the voice of one crying in the wilderness, an allusion to a lion.] [Luke's symbol is the ox, a sacrificial beast, and the book begins with the sacrifice of Zacharias.] [The prologue of John seems to soar on eagle's wings.] All these points are true, but they barely begin to portray the depth of meaning of the symbols of the four books. Such shallow interpretation is not the fault of the symbols themselves but rather our limited imagination.

Once we learn to immerse ourselves in free-flowing visualization, we begin to apprehend the fullness of meaning which was a common experience of pre-literate culture. Those of us with university degrees tend to be snobbish concerning illiterates, but all our educational honors would mean little if for the first time we were trying to follow a native through the dangerous trails of the Amazon rain forest. I am suggesting that in addition to all our book knowledge we need to relearn through meditation, relaxation techniques and visualizing symbols, how to open up the inner mind, so our lives can flow with more serenity, beauty, and effectiveness. Many of the little snarls, tripping over insignificant details, will be done away and in all our relationships we can enjoy a satisfaction long denied.

The Christian tradition is a priceless heritage to a major segment of humanity over two thousand years of history. At the same time we should recognize similar energies manifesting in other religious cultures around the globe. Among the Indians of North America we find an almost identical set of symbols. In their inner vision of the four energies they see the butterfly as air, the thunderbird as fire, the turtle earth, and the frog water. "Fire, air, earth, and water were the elder brethren of humankind, energies to be recognized and greeted with respect, the elementals of life which endowed the earth with power or 'wakanda,' as the Sioux Indians called the great mystery of the earth-spirits."[38] Terminology may vary from tribe to tribe, culture to culture, country to country, but basic energies remain the same.

It is the inner visions we own which prepare our future. If we seek hope for peace and harmony on planet earth, let us study our archetypal symbols from all cultures and religions. Finding the root pictures which cloak the basic energies we shall be surprised to find how much basic unity we share. So shall we build peace, not based on terrorizing nuclear power, but on inner rhythms of harmony which exist in the hearts of all humanity.

A NEW SENSE OF DESTINY

Chapter 10

Putting This Knowledge to Use

What can I do that a more vital and total perception both of my own inner workings and my relationship to those around me may be found? How can I refine my sense of vocation and personal destiny? Hopefully, some of the individuals who have studied this book up to this point will now wish more precise directions on how to put their knowledge to use. While there have been hints and suggestions in the chapters preceding, let us now try to be as specific as possible.

It is a fact that education in any of the civilized countries today requires much reading. Through long hours of assimilating books as our main thoroughfare to information we have probably narrowed the channeling process to the brain into a limited band which we call beta consciousness... roughly 13-30 cycles per second. This is something much less than true normal consciousness for human beings, but is the probable result of twelve years of public education and for many a great deal more years of studying books. To counter-act that narrowing down each one of us must find a new pathway which will somehow expand our channel of perceiving into a greater band-width. We must seek a technique which will cause our brain waves to actually slow down, yet at the same time become more powerful, as they will be both higher and deeper. This means moving into alpha 9-13 cps, or theta 7-8 cps. In these states we will be more alert, our memory on better recall, and our thinking process moving with greater clarity. As the majority of our readers will not have access to a brainwave EEG readout we can best describe this as a state of heightened awareness found in deep relaxation or a light trance. This is our goal.

For those persons who have been accustomed to gaining achievements through trying harder this new process of relaxed channeling will seem remarkably elusive. It does not involve a tightening of the screws on our mental and nervous system. It is the opposite... a letting go... the losing of frowns from the face... a healing laughter which lets the body and mind function at optimum level. If it seems beyond your capability, remember that what we are seeking to attain is actually our most natural state of being. All children have it... primitive people retain it through their lifetime. It is only a question of returning to what is our most natural life-style. This is the way God created us. It was an ancient Chinese custom to bind little girls' feet... presumably to make them more attractive. In wiser times the feet were allowed to grow as they should. In a similar way we are talking about removing tight wrappings, not from the feet, but from the mind.

It is my experience in dealing with hundreds of persons that there is no one technique which can be successfully used for all people. Essentially we are asking each individual to do whatever helps them to have the simplicity... the faith... of a child. What accomplishes this process will be different for various types of people. For seven years I directed a biofeedback stress control laboratory. From experience we learned that each person who walked into our door was unique. What worked for one might not work for another. Some liked to be talked to... others did not. Some were helped by quiet music... others were not. The most common approaches were through breathing and muscle relaxation exercises. Consciousness improvement is by no means limited to biofeedback laboratories. Though progress may be more at random, results can be had in a wide variety of situations. A service of worship in a church or synagogue may be the opening door to deeper consciousness. Others may find their opening up occurs during a walk in the woods or by the seaside. Some people find a great awakening occurring during a musical concert, while others may find their imagination stimulated and their perceptions sharpened through reading poetry.

As you attain a heightened state of awareness visualize your finest goals, those projects which can be of greatest benefit to the world. The vibrant power of such mental pictures held before the inner, mental eye will provide strong and lasting stimulus to action. By this process the best that God has given us will be engaged in satisfying usefulness. Many athletes have successfully used mental picturing of themselves winning a race, breaking a time or distance barrier. People enslaved to smoking picture themselves with clean lungs, renewed taste buds and healthier mouth till the picture becomes reality.

At the same time that we are learning to widen our bands of perception through what can be best described as "passive" alertness, we can also begin to read the style of those about us through symbols and so live in greater peace and harmony. We are all members of the human race. In our families we know moments of joy and times of despair. Our angry and upset times often come out of failing to understand and empathize with the essential style of those with whom we daily rub shoulders. Through regaining the insights of the lost language of alchemy and astrology our chances for building better relationships will be improved. With this knowledge we can quickly move from dissonance to harmony. Here are some suggestions for putting our awakened consciousness to immediate, practical use.

Get an astrological chart of yourself, and if possible of those people with whom you are closely associated. Reading from a birth certificate send the exact time and place of birth to an astrological computer service.[39] If that is not possible at least knowing another's birthday will give you their sun sign which is of some, but limited value. If you do not already have some knowledge of astrology read a few basic books from your library or bookstore. Acquaint yourself with this eloquent language by which the ancients sought to understand their relationship to each other and the planetary system. Now meditate on the alchemical concepts of air, fire, earth and water. Looking at your own chart and those of others see if the language doesn't express truths about the makeup of people whom you already know. Reading a chart of someone you are seeking to know can tell you a good deal about a person's essential style. When recruiting people for your organization this will be worth much in addition to the common dossier including education and job experience.

Beginning with air signs, if you need to solve intellectual problems get a Gemini. If the intellectual problems are of a delicate nature and require seeing all sides of the question with the promotion of peace and harmony... find a Libra. If there are problems to be solved which require dedication to the good of all humanity then an Aquarian is your choice.

If leadership is your problem... things are at a standstill, and need to be fired up... look to the fire sign people. An Aries will be the outstanding generator of new movements. A Leo will be the steady driver who keeps everlastingly at it till the job is done. The Sagittarian will use the flash of mind and voice to stimulate innovative thrusts.

If your daily existence has lacked down-to-earth practicality you need to absorb some earth sign people into your web of life. Your ideas, drive and emotions have not been fulfilled in terms of this-world accomplishments so now is the time to link with earth sign people. Those born under the sign of Taurus are the most basic. These are hard workers, tillers of the soil, admirers of the beauty of the natural world. They are most aware of the physical world all around them. Through all of the senses; sight, touch, hearing, taste and smell they have an acute appreciation of their surroundings. They relish creating beauty in art, architecture or their home atmosphere.

The Virgo, to all the physical awareness of the Taurus, adds the gift of organization. The Virgo works to make the world planned and predictable. For those whose lives always seem to be at loose ends fighting the chaos of disorganization the Virgo friend will be a gift of God. The Capricorn will quickly spot the useable plan... the routine which has practicality... clean out the loose ends and rubbish... giving one the sense that he is partaking in a plan which will work. If you have had what you thought was good down-to-earth planning, but in fact, it never went anywhere then solicit the aid of a Capricorn. To the natural instincts of the Taurus and Virgo, the Capricorn will add the ability of relating to the family, job or community situation. The Capricorn has the instinct for quietly and deftly making the right moves and connections to lead projects to success.

However, a good many of the most successful persons in the country, whose careers are the envy of all, still at some time in their lives become aware that they are missing an important dimension. Their daily life and long-range planning have the intellectual precision of a fine watch. In their roles as leaders they have ample opportunity to exert their fiery drive and move multitudes through their organizations. Furthermore, their lives are rounded out in solid, down-to-earth practicality. They own their homes and have surrounded themselves with things of physical beauty. Nevertheless, with all these attainments at some point they have become aware of an inner emptiness... somehow their deepest spiritual life has not been nurtured. If this is the case let them look to water sign friends and see what their gift can be.

The Cancer friends who are free with both tears and laughter can lead us into expressions of our emotions which

80

we hardly knew existed. There is no way one can be a dull stick in the company of a Cancer. Hungry or thirsty the Cancer friend will take care of you like the most concerned mother. But the nursing of the body is only symbolic of the deeper nursing of the emotions. Have there been dangerous edges to your life... tough areas into which you were afraid to look... find a Scorpio to help you see them straight on. This one is without fear and will give you the courage to enter into the most perilous pathways of existence. You may have to sit in silence for long times with the Scorpio but at last you will be rewarded to know that no area of life is too dangerous to be explored.

Are you up against a life or death situation? Have severe changes about you caused you to wonder about the ultimate meanings of life? Find a Pisces friend. These are the ones who explore the final ranges of experience... less through philosophy, more through intuition. Here is the mystic who is learning to accept and live with what can only be described as the incomprehensible comedy and tragedy of human existence. But watch where your Pisces friend is. His symbol is two fish... on the low side he can drag you down into a mass of negative emotion. But on the high side he, above all signs, can lead you into the magnificent harmonies of the Eternal Presence.

A NEW SENSE OF DESTINY

Chapter 11

The Door

To pass through a door is to have a change of experience. Especially is this true, not when we are going from one room to another within a house or building, but rather from an outer environment to an inner. We are stepping from the outside with its day and night, sunlight or starlight, uncontrolled weather hot or cold, wet or dry, to an inner controlled environment. Psychologically speaking much can happen to us as we step from the world outside to the world within. Perhaps nowhere is the change more precipitous than in stepping from the outer sunlit world of busy city streets to the beauteous "within" of a great cathedral.

I doubt if there is anyone who has held a greater appreciation of French cathedrals than the noted sculptor, Auguste Rodin. Here are a few of his sentences describing the extraordinary influences which impinge upon us as we step into a cathedral. "I open the door. What order! The idea of perfection is impressed upon my mind. What eternal foundations! And that architectural virtue which I love so much, that breadth so lacking in our epoch! Solidity and depth that survive the centuries! With passion I breathe this power. At the other end of the church the Holy of Holies is in darkness... only the gold of a hanging lamp glimmers. A large silence in which one feels the sages deliberating within themselves."[40]

Few persons love books more than I. I have acquired and read them by the hundreds and thousands. Books have had much to do with the make-up and direction of my mind. I can scarcely imagine what my world would be without books. But I never have opened and read a book with anything like the total experience of opening the door of a cathedral. At such a moment, a lost symbolic language in architecture, in stained glass windows, in statuary and art... riding on the vibrations of music from that greatest of instruments, the organ... chanting choirs... light and shade moving and changing with the rising and lowering of the position of the sun... acts upon us in such a way that our total person becomes involved.

My first experience as a young man entering a major cathedral was at St. John the Divine in New York City. Leaving the busy, noisy streets of Manhattan I opened the door; the magnificent display of light and shadow around the great pillars and aisles, the music of the organ practicing softly in the distance, left me with only one plausible response... to go to my knees in prayer. As on few occasions in my life... I felt my entire being involved. Mind and emotions, physical body and spiritual strength were singing in perfect harmony. This is the power of the lost language of ancient symbolism which was created to be a channel of the Holy Spirit for the "uneducated" masses of the Middle Ages.

May that minority of persons who live in the vicinity of beautiful cathedrals go again and again seeking to comprehend in their beings the full-band perception of the experience of prayer, blissfully aided by the rainbow hues of sunlight streaming through magnificent stained glass. May they experience both intellectually and emotionally the stories from the Bible as skillfully executed in sculpture, painting and glass. May they be so fortunate as to be lifted up by the strains of beautiful music written in praise of God, sung by choirs, and articulated by great pipe organs.

The majority of us will have but occasional opportunity for such creative worship. However, this same majority has access to thousands of books in libraries and bookstores. Perhaps you are wondering if I am suggesting that the normal practice of reading a book is an almost total loss for full-band perception of reality. In fact, for many it has been exactly that. In the process of reading over hundreds of thousands of printed pages we have dulled our wider range of perceptive faculties. Nevertheless, at this point I want to say as strongly as I can that books can be a powerful tool for full range perception of life in all its dimensions, colors, sounds, odors, with impact on mind and heart. With books we can follow the minds of thousands of authors into a multitude of experiences which could never be ours. However, our personal reading may conjure up only a pale silhouette of their experience. To get what any good book has the potential of giving us, we must enlist the fullness of our imagination as our eyes follow the lines on the page.

In the present century we have become knowledgeable as never before concerning the mechanics of the process of seeing. We have cleverly constructed glasses and contact lenses to clarify the seeing process. We have the skills to restore seeing by removing foggy cataracts. We have learned ways to reduce the pressure of glaucoma. Most recently we have enlisted the fantastic skills of laser beam surgery to perform remarkably delicate reconstruction within the eyeball. All of these new techniques are welcome news to those persons whose eyesight is threatened. Yet these techniques, important though they are, have little to do with the most significant part of the seeing process. There is a seeing with the mind which is something more than receiving the optical message from the nervous system by which the eyes are connected to the brain.

George K. Lovgren has written a remarkable little book titled THE ART OF INNER SEEING. In his foreword The Gift We Are Squandering, he says... "The light source that illumines what we see with our eyes closed; our dreams, mental outpicturing, pictorial memories, etc., must have been with us since long before any light from the outside came to our awareness. It actuated our existence in our predawn biological morning before we had either eyes or brain. It constituted our thought, guided our progress and brought us unerringly to today's tremendous success. The inner light did not abandon us when we invented the eyes – it is still our central 'I'. It is an intrinsic determinant within our thought forming process – it maintains, renews and represents itself throughout our life-activity. It is the area operandum of the visionary."[41]

Let us keep our books. Let us continue to follow the many exciting pathways into which authors can lead us. But as we go we must not let our senses become dulled by the myriads of words on a page. Let us take with us "the art of inner seeing," letting our imaginations have full range. With each group of words passing before our eyes may mental images appear in living color on the screen of the inner mind.

How many of us have read a book and declared to friends what a dull work it was. At another time we hear an excited reviewer, someone who has learned to cherish the contents of this same book, give an interpretation of the author's work in a way which we find tremendously stimulating. How was this possible? The answer is simple. The reviewer had used the inner imagination. We had not. The reviewer was vitally recapturing what the author had seen in the mind's eye. Our minds had merely trudged wearily over ink and paper with no significant visualization. Books can continue to be an open door into many wonderful experiences, but only if we develop the art of inner seeing. George Lovgren tells us how to do this.

"Let us close our eyes and look with real intent to see. There is, as you so well know, a mumble jumble of pictures like a disorganized and meaningless movie theatre. It has always been there, but you have long since been weaned of paying attention to it. Your education took care of that. Perhaps you did not know that this picture parade is going on all the time, given attention or not, eyes closed and just as well with open eyes. You cannot see the pictures with open eyes, just as you cannot see stars in daylight – although, the pictures exist even when you do not look at them, and influence everything that enters your eyes and occupies your mind, much as planets affect our earth's equilibrium even when unseen. As you look at this inner world, it enlivens, as if grateful for your attention. The more you look, the more you see, and the more interest you give it, the livelier it becomes."[42]

It is possible to memorize books, but this may be nothing more than mechanically parroting words from a page. If we will learn to use the art of inner seeing we can come close to recreating before the mind's eye the reality which the author saw. Probably we will read more slowly. Perhaps we shall read a few lines and then turn away from the page letting our thoughts drift. Sometimes inward visions will exhibit themselves with a reality that shocks us. Now we are beginning to achieve that vital and total perception which belonged to so many of the worshipers in the cathedrals in the pre-Gutenberg days. In the same fashion as people leaving busy city streets to open the door to the peace and beauty of cathedral aisles,... let us open the door of the inner mind as we read great books. By so doing we can receive treasured experiences we had not thought possible.

A NEW SENSE OF DESTINY

Chapter 12

Bridging the Gulf between East and West

One of the themes of this book is the proposition that with twelve years of public education as a general minimum and continued reading of books, magazines and newspapers, we have acquired vast sums of knowledge, but have done so at the expense of the use of a much broader band of consciousness. In fairness to the total culture of the planet it should be said that this particular style of manifestation of education is to be identified primarily with the Western world. Its style began with ancient Greece and was reborn after the Dark Ages with the Renaissance, but on the whole is alien to the East.

The East characteristically has never succumbed to the thought that education is marked, not by our depth of knowing, but rather by how great a number of areas of studies are our arena regardless of the shallowness of that knowing. Looking at the globe in terms of studies of the human brain, the left hemisphere is likened to the intellectual West, while the East is in the manner of the intuitive right hemisphere. Our inability to understand the true nature of the gulf that separates us is caused by a major difference in manner of perception. This is the root cause of sad conflicts, and sometimes bloody wars, between the people of America and Europe and their brothers and sisters in Asia.

Dr. Abraham M. Rihbany reminds us that the culture and language of the Near East has developed a style that can be confusing to Western minds. In his THE SYRIAN CHRIST we read, "A Syrian's chief purpose in a conversation is to convey an impression by whatever suitable means, and not to deliver his message in scientifically accurate terms. He expects to be judged not by what he says, but by what he means… It is also because the Syrian loves to speak in pictures, and to subordinate literal accuracy to the total impression of an utterance, that he makes such extensive use of figurative language… Just as the Oriental (Easterner) loves to flavor his food strongly and to dress in bright colors, so is he fond of metaphor, exaggeration, and positiveness in speech. To him mild accuracy is weakness."[43]

In view of continuing hostilities between Eastern and Western nations in the Near East it is easy to see how there can be misunderstandings even when there is accurate translation of words. In the simple matter of greetings Dr. Rihbany describes the Syrian style. "You have greatly honored me by coming into my home. I am not worthy of it. It is a blessing to have you under my roof; your presence makes our day three times as happy. This house is yours; you can burn it if you wish. My children also are at your disposal; I would sacrifice them all to your pleasure."[44] This is simply an ornate way of saying, "I'm glad to see you." Not for a moment would it be taken seriously, literally to burn the house down and sacrifice the children.

To Western minds, if we fail to communicate accurately with Oriental nations, we naturally assume that it is a matter of mistranslation. Western diplomats and businessmen have false confidence in believing that all problems will be solved simply by seeing that highly skilled translators are used, and that they are checked on to see if they have done their job correctly. This is a fatal misunderstanding. It will be the cause of angry verbal quarrels, possibly tragic international events, bringing us to the brink of new wars. It will be doomed to widening the gulf between East and West. What is the answer?

The answer is subtle; not easily appreciated by the average Western mind. Yet, to build that necessary bridge of fluid, accurate flow of communications between Orient and Occident, it must be grasped and put to use. Our problem, which has divided us, is more than a simple failure to comprehend the precise meaning of each other's words. The real nature of the predicament is that we are attempting to talk while coming in on different wavelengths. It is as though we were insisting that we could listen to an FM broadcast with an AM radio. No matter how much you twist the dial, it's not going to work. The Oriental mind is accustomed to using a rich symbolism which is sent and received on a broader band of perception than is commonly used by Western minds.

We complain that the Orientals are easily upset... become so emotional... over certain words we use. What we must learn to understand is that those listeners in other parts of the world are receiving on a much wider band of perception. They sense and feel overtones in our words of which we are totally unaware. Simply striving for more accurate translation, while failing to become aware that the entire manner of perception is involved, fails to solve the problem. The Near East is today, and has long been, an arena of international conflicts. At the beginning of attempts to deal with the countries of the Islamic tradition we need to get to the root of our two different styles of communication. We must learn to grasp that every symbol used by the Arabic mind is freighted with a host of additional implications... some of which are perceived in intuitive and emotional ways foreign to our normal comprehension.

As the Bible was created at the vortex of the Levant, in the distinctive manner of the Near East, using it for an example of interpretation can be helpful. Educated Western minds often fail to comprehend the fullness of what is said. For example, both Matthew and Luke's gospels tell of Jesus calling disciples when one of them says, "Lord, let me first go and bury my father."[45] Jesus seems to reply in uncharacteristic, brutal harshness, "Follow me, and leave the dead to bury their own dead."[46] We recoil at the thought that Jesus wants us to be so busy following his ways that we can't take time to attend our own father's funeral. Isn't this contrary to the commandment, "Honor thy father and thy mother"?[47] But those who know the world of the Near East are aware that the expression, "Let me first go and bury my father," did not mean that the father was about to die. Rather it meant that the son was to be at home taking care of family affairs over what might be many years until his father's death, then he would come and be a follower of Jesus. Jesus felt this was too long a delay.

For another example from the Bible, writing in the 8th century B.C. a Hebrew prophet, Isaiah, had a vision of that day when...

"they shall beat their swords into plowshares,
and their spears into pruning hooks...". [48]

To a literal, beta-conscious Western mind these words would state nothing more than their surface value... swords can be converted into plowshares... spears can be beaten into pruning hooks. Those who know the Oriental symbolic ways of thought interpret these lines in far more general fashion. They would understand that the entire machinery of warfare is to be converted into an educational and cultural mechanism for building peace between nations; not just "spears becoming pruning hooks," but the diversion of personnel and finance from the machinery of war to the channels of peace.

Dr. Zamenhov, a Russian physician and scholar, in the year 1887, seeking to bridge international language barriers, gave the world Esperanto. Blending the European languages by dropping out the unusual and keeping the grammar simple, Esperanto opened a channel of communication which was much easier than learning several national languages. However, this lacked significance for those languages of the Orient and Africa which have little or no relationship to the European tongues. Esperanto means "hope," and it was a step in the right direction. It is our conviction that communication through symbols offers even greater hope. Even as mathematics is the same in every country, so too picture-symbols are an open way for precise, meaningful communication. A tree, a mountain, a river, a person, a dog, the sun, the rain, these are the same in all countries and with pictures of them we can express ourselves meaningfully.

Further, we need to emphasize that symbolic language is more than just another among many national tongues; more than just an attempt at a universal language. Symbolic language communicates at deeper levels of meaning. Standing at the foot of Mt. Rushmore in the Black Hills of South Dakota looking up at the larger than life sculpture of four presidents, Washington, Jefferson, Lincoln and Theodore Roosevelt in glistening granite, framed by dark pines, one can sense that the visitors coming from many walks of life are finding united inspiration. From this moment of vision visitors will carry home indelible memories building a deeper patriotism. There is something here that even people of other countries and other tongues can appreciate. This is an opening up of communication on wider bands of perception, heart and soul, as well as mind. For two nations with Christian roots, the Christ of the Andes standing high in the mountains between Argentina and Chile, has long served to encourage peaceful borders.

The world reaches out for symbols of unity of all nations. The photo taken from outer space of our blue planet with white clouds hanging fragilely in the interplanetary abyss may be our best symbol. To look on that picture has enormous overtones of concern for our environment, the unity of nations, and world peace. It is no surprise that youth of all countries, fearful of their future in a nuclear age, have placed this picture of the blue planet on their walls as a sign of concern for peace among all people preserving our planetary home for future generations. With symbols such as this we have the instrumentation for building the bridge that so often separates East and West. With it we are able to tune in on an identical wavelength as speakers and listeners.

The worst barrier which stands high, almost impenetrable, is of our own creation. It exists in the assumption that we in the high-tech, industrially rich and successful West are superior. There is no need to build a bridge… just let the other nations come our way, by whatever means they can, as they learn how superior we are. The fact is that the superiority of our industrial machine is in shambles. Furthermore, students with high school international scholarships, free to go to any nation, choose the U.S. only if they want the easy way. The schools of other nations are acknowledged to be more difficult, but with prospects of better, more complete education. Youthful Japanese hoping for a future in technology, industry, and banking are more willing to undergo the discipline of learning English than our college youth to master an Oriental tongue. Western superiority in education and industrial efficiency can no longer be presumed to be a fact. If we cannot on our own be humble, it is becoming apparent that the facts of life will soon force us to do so.

S. Radhakrishnan whose personal life bridged East and West for he was both a professor at Oxford University and Vice-President of the Republic of India writing in 1939 spoke eloquently on the need of this century. "The supreme task of our generation is to give a soul to the growing world-consciousness, to develop ideals and institutions necessary for the creative expression of the world soul, to transmit these loyalties and impulses to future generations and train them into world citizens."[49]

Hopes for the accomplishment of this noble task lie in the rebirth of the symbolic lost language of pre-Gutenberg times adding new symbols pertinent to the rising consciousness of our New Age. Total planetary communication on wide band perception can best be attained with the use of an imaginative vocabulary of pictorial symbols which grasp heart and soul as well as mind.

A NEW SENSE OF DESTINY

Chapter 13

How Important Is Symbolic Language?

Life is filled with interesting subjects. In newspapers, magazines, and books it is easy to read of hundreds of fascinating hobbies from the collecting of shells to the study of stars. We can enjoy photography or painting. We may weave rugs, or see how many varieties of dahlias we can grow. While we may hear of such pursuits, and believe we would enjoy them, in fact, we pass most of them by. Symbols, pictures filled with psychological content, the lost language of the preliterate world, are they worth serious study, or do we now pass on to other things?

I suppose that everyone feels that their particular interest is of great consequence, or else they would not be giving it a major part of their time. Nevertheless, I seek to show that recovery of the lost language should be of extraordinary importance to every human being. The Chinese have told us that one picture is worth a thousand words. The Sufi mystics have taught us that one symbol can be read on several different levels of thought. Modern psychologists say that symbols can accomplish more complete communication between persons than mere words. Further, they are teaching us that symbols can open up understanding between the conscious and the subconscious mind. The content of our dreams, those inner pictures of our sleeping hours, are being taken more seriously for revealing the direction of our lives.

Inner seeing is not just another hobby we might pick up from time to time. Inner seeing is our "vital life." It is the center of our total consciousness. To use a symbol, this inner seeing may be likened to the sun from which energy flows to the planets of the solar system. The thesis of our book is that we have robbed the central sun of its natural power to cause us to be, and do, because we are overshadowed with a wearying network of words. Trying to read every serious commentator on the vast multitude of subjects worthy of our attention, we have succumbed to mental fatigue, and lost our powers of inner imaging. Depressed with paper-thin experiences of living, we seek release through drugs and alcohol. The answer lies not in suppression of shallow, unsatisfying living, but in opening up the potential vitality of the image making process which lies at the central core of every person.

Dr. Hans Selye of Montreal was for many years the leading teacher concerning the effects of stress upon the human body. He stated that the vast array of human illnesses, which have been induced by stress, can include everything from headaches to ulcers, arthritis to colitis, and hypertension to general fatigue. In modern society too many of us live under constant stress. We need breaks from the continual "push." But, surprisingly, his final answer is not that we be removed from stress-inducing situations. His summation of the matter is that we should go to our innermost source of light and guidance. Our bodies and minds are really not as tired as they seem to be.

We are tired, stressed, because our minds are caught in the crossfire of directives from other people. We are tired, and beginning to show bodily signs of breakdown, because we have not dared to do what WE want to do. Selye says that the key to release our inner strength is to decide for ourselves what we really want to do, and then do it with all our might. "... it won't hurt you to work hard for something you want, but make sure that it is really you who wants it – not merely your society, parents, teachers, neighbors..."[50] "... your principal aim should be not to avoid work but to find the kind of occupation which, for you, is play."[51]

A NEW SENSE OF DESTINY

Dr. Selye in his studies has seen people who have broken many of the rules of good health... they eat poor diets, don't exercise, fail to get enough sleep... but nevertheless live happily into late years. Why, because they are caught up in doing things which they truly enjoy. This releases the powerful energies from the innermost being. These high vitality people can be described in numerous ways. Psychologists would say that such happy people have a true union between the depths of the subconscious mind and the programming of everyday activities. Students of mind process would say that right and left hemispheres of the brain are working in perfect harmony. Biofeedback therapists would declare that such fortunate persons have learned to disdain the narrow track of beta-consciousness and are enjoying the fullness of unity between thoughts and feelings in deep alpha-consciousness. In common parlance we would say that these people have "got it all together." Mystics would proclaim that such people have tapped the "God-within."

Symbolic language is the perfect tool for bringing the far corners of our personal experience into a comprehensive unity. As such it is not just something for the dilettante who is looking for a new thing to occupy time for the moment. Rather, it is of greatest importance in helping us to come alive to the fullness of our potential. How many of our days have been only boredom, ennui, for lack of any gathered, vital events; a bit of housework, sitting in a traffic jam, dreary hours at a desk, perhaps a few moments of concentration, but much too much of trivial pursuit in our daily routine.

Kenneth R. Pelletier in his TOWARD A SCIENCE OF CONSCIOUSNESS shows how foolish have been our fragmented efforts at trying to deal with the full range of any individual's being. "In Western culture, man has been conceptualized as having a separate body, mind, and spirit. The body-mind-spirit division is readily evidenced in the structure of the healing professions. Physicians are dedicated to the treatment of the body; psychiatrists and psychologists are concerned with treating the mind; and yet a third group, the clergy, is attendant to the soul, or spiritual healing. These areas tend to be discrete and antagonistic."[52]

Fortunately, a new movement is coming to birth in the healing arts called "holistic" medicine. An individual is not just a "gall-bladder," a "psychotic" or a "sinner." He is one person whose body, mind and soul are inextricably interrelated. What happens in any one part affects all the rest. Indicative of the depth of the fragmentation is the observation that to the lay-person the languages used by the doctor, the psychologist, and the theologian are equally an impossible barrier.

Symbols, however, more than written words, communicate with deeper levels of being. They are the instrument by which our dreams enable our conscious thoughts to examine the deeper reality of the subconscious. Any individual who can learn to communicate with different levels of his own being will be better prepared to live effectively and harmoniously with others. Comparing inward visions and the symbols they attract with those of our friends and associates will teach us much wisdom in human relations.

The noted musician, philosopher, and astrologer, Dane Rudhyar writes... "To such a perfected intuitive man no particular system of symbolism is necessary; and astrology is of no special value. But he cannot communicate his intuitions to others. Communication necessitates a system of interpretation; a set of symbols which can serve as spatial-mental 'bridges' between the wholeness of the moment and all perceivers. It thus needs a language. Astrology is such a language, just as the series of hexagrams of the Chinese I Ching is such a language. And it is in the formation and use of such a language that what we call holistic logic and the principle of functional coherency come into operation."[53]

97

A NEW SENSE OF DESTINY

The lost languages of astrology and alchemy can mark the beginning of a full range language of symbolism by which modern humanity has hope for open communication between all nations of the planet earth. At the same time there will be a better understanding of the inner depths of each one of us with a greater release of our total dynamic. Do these thoughts incline us to see how necessary it is that today's world learns again the lost language?

A NEW SENSE OF DESTINY

Chapter 14

Enter the Computer

No up-to-date book seeking to develop communication skills, and attempting to involve the whole person in the process, would be dealing fairly with the subject while bypassing the computer. Spanning the recorded history of mankind three obvious, almost incredible leaps have taken place. Shrouded in the unrecorded mists of time simple symbols, hieroglyphs, gradually became written languages. As time went on in order to save effort the picture symbols were produced in abbreviated form but still carried the same message. This speeded-up simplification occurred in Egypt during the First Dynasty and is known as "hieratic" writing. An even further simplification known as "demotic" brought us to a close approximation of the written languages of today. From the simplest picture carved on a rock as a way-sign to the traveler, to the beautifully involved nuances of the ancient Greek language for the expression of poetry, drama and history, this first stage, the development of a written language, was a vast leap in the growth of civilization.

The second major acceleration took place with the invention of the printing press placing books on an extraordinary variety of topics in the hands of vast multitudes. As a part of this huge paradigm shift in the educational process in addition to the sale of books by the millions, the civilized countries created public schools and free libraries. Until this time general illiteracy was the assumed state of affairs for mankind. Now the majority of the human race could participate in the educational process. We have tried to explain that in some ways this was not a bargain. While any individual now might become conversant with thousands of sub-

99

jects this same person's in-depth "knowing" often became shallow and meaningless. But against that loss was the fantastic expansion of knowledge, no longer in the minds of a tiny minority of royalty, priests, and scholars, but now a boiling up of intellectual growth in the great masses of all civilized nations.

Finally, within the past decade, the human race has entered a third major leap forward, a wide-scale encounter with the computer. While it is much too early to assess the total impact of this invention, we can at least begin to evaluate both its gains and losses for the human race. The computer's most obvious gain, the ability to process and relate enormous amounts of highly complex data in brief moments of time, and to send and receive as part of national and world-wide networks, has already begun to develop so many applications that an entire library could be written on this subject. All phases of the civilized world, economic, military, educational, political, even religious are involved in the technological changeover.

Those still uninitiated into this new world may be unaware that entirely new languages have already been created to do justice to the full potential of computers. Not content with BASIC we have more powerful languages for specific purposes; FORTRAN for science and engineering, COBOL for business programming. Beyond these there is the high-level Pascal which is able to manipulate data for faster program execution. Dozens of other new languages are in process of creation to serve specific needs. When we think that both the hardware and software in daily use today was unknown as recently as a decade ago we can scarcely imagine what the next decade, much less the next century, will bring.

As this book deals with astrological symbolism, and I have referred earlier to the need for this subject to undergo broad scientific verification, I would like at this point to give a quotation from Rob Hand, a pioneer in the use of computers in astrology. "The computer is the most important tool to come along for astrology in its entire history. The microcomputer, accessible to almost all, is the form which will have the greatest impact on astrology. This is our microscope, our particle accelerator. In the past it could be argued that astrology lacked the proper tools to prove its case and establish itself as a true science. This is no longer the case. We have what we need. It is only a matter of our learning how to use this and other tools and of applying ourselves to the work. We may have to give up many cherished ideas about astrology in the process, but I have no doubt that the fundamental principle of astrology, the interaction of human symbolism, consciousness and the cosmos will come out of this work intact. Astrology is a subject with revolutionary potential for humanity. The microcomputer is the tool that will make the potential into the actual."[54]

I have little doubt but that parts of astrology, such as newspaper columnists grinding out bland prescriptions on what to expect and do each day for the different sun signs, will soon be replaced with far more precise interpretations. These better renderings will be accomplished because the computer can give each individual a complete chart, not acting simply from the sun sign, but showing one's total sensitivities. Furthermore, large scale population studies checking signs against observed human nature will tell us what is true and what is false in the assumptions of ancient astrology.

At the same time we are just beginning a careful charting of all the geo-cosmic energies which have their influence upon human life. Not only the familiar forces of gravity, heat and cold, rainy or arid climates, wind or calm, but the more subtle fields of electricity and magnetism, both those created by man and those naturally occurring from sun, moon, our solar system, our galaxie and the universe will be shown to continually fashion and change life on earth. What is the actual relationship between sunspots and changing times and life-styles on earth? How do the Van Allen radiation belts trap and release cosmic forces producing planetary changes? What of the changing forces on the solar system as it moves in a helix through our galaxie?

Or turning from macro-cosmic effects to the microcosmic, how is it that the "green-thumb" of a true plant lover causes seed to germinate more quickly and develop larger and healthier plants? Are there measurable forces involved in healing effects of prayer, not only on the mind but also the physical body? We have been occasionally challenged by anecdotes of miraculous cures; with the computer these can be placed and evaluated in wide-scale studies. Computer networks are already making the latest results of medical research immediately available to hospitals and doctors as they work with new and unusual cases. The youth of today stand at the beginning of a new age with the microcomputer being the remarkable tool available for charting all the subtle relationships between each person and the total surrounding environment.

Standing at the vantage point of many centuries of history we know the extraordinary importance of both the written word and the availability to the masses of printed books. If the computer is the third revolutionary force in the ever-increasing speed of human competence, what will be its reasonable parameters? Are we in some ways expecting too much of this fabulous invention? Probably of greatest importance are the tasks to which it can be addressed which will deal most directly with the pressing needs of a troubled, fragile world with its starving millions, a world-wide arms race threatening to destroy the economies of not only the major nations, but also the Third World countries. Can the computer help us to solve the dilemma of sudden nuclear destruction, or the slower death of pollution of the environment?

I don't for a moment believe that some great scientist is going to create a program that feeds into an enormous computer all the equations of life, and that the answers will come forth on a print-out. Even if this did happen there would still be the greater problem of the implementation of the answers. However, at the top of our list of the contributions of the computer we should place one which is purely psychological. In time of great need humanity has available an extraordinary new tool.

According to an ancient Biblical story, at the time of the destruction of much of mankind by rains and water, Noah's Ark successfully sailed over the flood till dry ground could be found. In later times an invention occurred which may more closely approximate our current situation. At first sailors did not dare to venture beyond the sight of land for fear of being unable to return to safe harbors. Later they learned to navigate on the open seas by sun and stars. Still there remained a fearful enemy, fog, and clouds obscuring the guide points of the skies. Under leaden heavens many a ship foundered on rocky coasts with the loss of the mariners' lives. Then a life-saving invention, the magnetic compass, gave the ships' navigators eyes to continue their journeys through the darkest nights and most dense fogs. With the compass and ever more carefully drawn navigational charts the forbidding seas became open passage-ways to all points of the globe. The ocean lanes would not be traveled without fears, yet at the same time the pilots could now enjoy a comfortable sense of place and destination.

Even as the ark met a need, and the compass another, so in our fearful times the computer can give us psychological comfort and hope. On the one hand this is purely emotional... the knowledge that in crises of disaster humanity always seems to come up with resources which could not have been imagined in our fathers' times. On the other hand the computer is truly giving us chart and compass to plot out a better way for life on the planet. Through this remarkable device we can create graphs of population growth, and from them can plot necessary food resources. Through computers we can rapidly chart the effects of environmental pollution and what will be required to restore the land. While knowledge of the problem is by no means the complete answer, nevertheless a skilled knowledge of the problems about us can show where we are able to most effectively apply needed change.

In our hours of most extreme optimism is it possible that we are expecting too much from our computers? Because we can already log the extraordinary accomplishments of this device; we could not have walked on the moon, sent rockets to the planets sending back information about them, brought all of science and business into a new era of rapid accomplishments without them; perhaps we have begun to expect too much. The area most open to philosophic discussion involves the question of creating artificial intelligence. Flushed with current accomplishments, and with hopes of even greater magnitude already on our horizon such as elimination of diseases which have long plagued mankind, or the building of communities in space where completely new styles of civilization might be born, some are asking, "Has the computer given birth to an artificial intelligence which exceeds the known limits of the human species?"

In the halls of high-tech writers of creative software an earnest debate on this subject has already begun. Prior to our current decade such thoughts were voiced only by the authors of science fiction. The optimists declare that we must not in any way think of putting limitations on the potential. A minority tends to be more guarded. The most complicated computers as compared with man still have a missing dimension.

"Consciousness" is an obvious clue word. While the computer can handle long strings of symbols and rearrange them for a great variety of uses, it can hardly be said to "be alive" in ways that we describe as "human." It seems to most closely resemble what we call the "idiot savant," who is a person utterly unable to function in normal ways in the social order, but is nevertheless able to do fantastic mathematical feats. While computers can be programmed to drive mechanical robots to do a wide variety of simple tasks, many of which were formerly done by humans, this is still a long way from what it means to be a fully conscious personality. In summation, we should say that the computer is going to be an extraordinary helper to mankind, not its replacement.

Especially in the light of the thesis of A NEW SENSE OF DESTINY we should note that in the new day of computer-human relationships the need for human beings to rediscover and expand the symbolic vocabulary of the ancients will exist more than ever. Too many hours in school and long hours reading have caused us to sometimes lose our imaginative faculty. We can see this on the brain wave monitor. A pre-school child is normally in alpha and theta state with slow, powerful brain waves, highly perceptive to everything. Some years later that same child will usually be in a narrow band of beta-consciousness, less broadly perceptive. A child gazing out the window may be told, "Stop day dreaming!" Yet it is exactly that kind of consciousness which has been the working style of some of our most creative geniuses. While learning to use a computer can in some ways be an exciting event, it is quite possible too many hours before a CRT may cause severe drying up of the imaginative faculty. Symbolic language on the other hand teaches the mind to use all of its height and depth, senses of color, taste and sound. The computer can be a remarkable servant... a genie... but symbolic language will serve a greater purpose, which is to help each one of us attain full stature as a physical, mental and spiritual being unified in one person.

105

A NEW SENSE OF DESTINY

Chapter 15

With All the Skills What Do We Say?

With our enhanced communication skills is it possible that we may be like the person who buys a car, but then can't decide where to drive it, and it simply remains in the garage? The majority of people buying new cars will find places to go. Perhaps they will just go for rides, cruising around, enjoying the new vehicle. This is bound to take them to some exciting places with scenes they have never previously witnessed. Just "cruising around" getting the feel of the language of alchemy and astrology will immediately afford fresh insights into nuances of character of the people about us.

Speaking of a forthright friend of ours who is an Aries we will exclaim, "Now I know why he has such a fiery personality!" Or discovering that the quiet treasurer of our company is a Virgo with moon in Capricorn we understand how he is so obviously in the right place. With the Virgo instinct for organization he would be certain that the books are in perfect order. With Capricorn moon he would be quietly rising to the top spot based on his qualifications. The schoolteacher trying to hold down a child who just "must" speak out on every subject will have more sympathy if she knows that she is dealing with the natural style of a Sagittarian. The husband married to a Cancer wife should forget that she has less aptitude for neatness and be grateful that she is always a good provider.

After getting acquainted with our new vocabulary, as we begin to enjoy the new insights we are receiving, it is natural that we ask ourselves, "What can these skills hope to accomplish in dealing with the seemingly insoluble issues of our times?" Let's examine human existence on planet earth. The current population is about four billion persons. By the year two thousand, based on current projections, the population will be over six billion. The birthrate per thousand in the United States today is fifteen, whereas in Third World countries that figure stands in the thirties or forties, two or three times our growth rate. Bangladesh with a birthrate of 47 per thousand population expects to grow from 85,000,000 to 153,000,000 by the end of the century. Mexico with a present population of almost 67 million will probably grow to 135 million by the year 2,000. Countries like Liberia and Ghana have the highest birthrates in the world.

It is obvious that with famine already prevalent in many parts of the earth our growing population will rapidly multiply this problem. Our planet may soon be the scene of nations armed to the teeth, locked in a death struggle, fighting for the resources of the earth. Should we be able to avoid warfare there is still the danger of bringing about a world unfit for further human existence. Already we have subjected air, water and soil to dangerous pollutants. Lifeless ponds testify to slow death from industry's acid rain. Nuclear war would be an unbelievable horror; the long-range effects of radiation might cast a death spell on humanity from which there can be no recovery. The late Margaret Mead has declared, "We won't have a society if we destroy the environment."[55] Paul Ehrlich has warned that if we don't take major steps to turn things around, "We shall eventually find ourselves stranded in space on a dead Spaceship Earth with no place to go and no way to get there."[56]

In the face of such impending catastrophes does it seem that playing with outmoded languages as a possible solution is the height of folly? "Let's be more realistic!," many would cry. I reply that I am being realistic. Nothing will have more to do with our future than those images of what we consider "reality" continually held before our eyes.

A NEW SENSE OF DESTINY

If we permit the problems to loom so large that all we can see is gloom and despair, then we have lost the energy to try to recover. If we can lift up before the mind's eye what at first seem small solutions, use them and develop them to deal with larger and larger scale problems, then there is hope. Then we can believe that the God who brought us thus far in creation is not going to let the experiment with humanity perish in sad scenes of warfare and famine. Again and again throughout human history when things looked impossible, somewhere a few persons were granted an inward vision of a better way. They followed that vision, let it grow and grow, till it became a power for themselves and others; they shook off their fears and despair, and lifted the world to a better plane of existence.

This is not just "wild-eyed idealism." Leaders in several nations becoming aware of the monumental dangers of overpopulation held up a vision before their people of the happiness of a country with only a slight rate of growth. Posters all over China of a joyful one child family, plus government incentives and restrictions, have caused the most numerous country in the world to radically reduce its rate of growth. Steps are being taken by many countries such as India to reduce birth rates. Voluntary cooperation within the United States has brought the birthrate down more rapidly than we had dared hope a decade or two ago. A vision we must continue to lift up is that of a world population which will not exceed our planet's potential living room. Only as such a vision is seen and held can we prevent the dangers of starvation, disease, and fighting for living room.

In the area of warfare we must vision a world community. We have lived too long with a mental picture of ourselves as a little national or ethnic group within our stockade ready to shoot down any enemies coming nearby. One of our worst problems has been the false visions we have had of each other as nations. If our view of competitive nations is seeing them as evil empires threatening to do us in, then we shall arm and arm until we either destroy each other in violent combat or collapse from within, no longer able to sustain the enormous cost of continually building new and more fantastic armaments. Can we see that the initial vision is the problem? With the tools of deeper symbolic language we can probe through those false visions of each other. Holding up a vision of the planet as one community we can begin communication between our respective countries which is not only mind to mind, but also heart to heart. We will begin to see that we as humans are all the same, that we need not be enemies, but can be friends. We are brothers and sisters whose long term goals – equality, justice, prosperity and peace – are sought by all.

Dane Rudhyar in his ASTROLOGY OF PERSONALITY shows the possible healing effects of the use of the lost language. "The man who is enmeshed in the continual warfare of primordial and natural elements finds in life nothing but chaos and chance; from which results fear. The man who sees these elements as functional parts of a cosmic whole, harmonized by outwardly complex, yet inherently simple laws of 'functional coherency,' overcomes fear. Having conceived and realized the universe as a whole, his life as a whole, his psyche and his body as a whole, he is able to ultimately identify himself with the wholeness of these wholes; and to stand in the abstract and 'mystical' relation of wholeness to whole."[57]

The recognition of the oneness of all humanity is carried to a greater degree by the insights of recent physics. Whereas Newtonian physics described matter and energy as two totally different entities, Einstein showed that each could become the other. Bell's Theorem declared that no particle in the universe could move without affecting every other particle in existence. David Bohm declares, "So we are led to propose further that the more comprehensive, deeper, and more inward actuality is neither mind nor body but rather a yet higher-dimensional actuality, which is their common ground and which is of a nature beyond both. Each of these is then only a relatively independent sub-totality and it is implied that this relative independence derives from the higher-dimensional ground in which mind and body are ultimately one."[58]

It is no wonder that the children of recent decades who were brought up to believe in small-scale behaviorism heard a fundamental note from ancient astrology and responded. Why did they read books on the stars and planets, decorate their rooms with signs of the zodiac, and adopt the ancient symbolic language? Having falsely been brought up in a thought world which assumed their lives were clay molded by parents and teachers, they inwardly knew their destiny was somehow related to the universe; gladly they threw off the old small-scale interpretation. The Christian story of the first Christmas has many facets that have captured the imagination... a valued child whose birth occurred in a stable... the love for a tiny baby... the devotion of Joseph and Mary... but certainly one note that continued to capture the imagination even during the most bleak times of rationalism was the story of the three kings, the Magi. These wise men came long miles across the desert following a rare sign in the sky, Saturn and Jupiter almost conjunct in the constellation of Pisces, to worship at the manger in Bethlehem. This ancient story held to the truth that our destiny is linked to the stars. Our youth recognized this story was telling them human lives are meaningful in the context of the universe; behind it all there is an ultimate being who cares about us and seeks to guide us to a better way. Though Herod would brutally kill all the little children in Bethlehem, Jesus would survive, and in the same way in the midst of a thousand tragic events the cosmic Creator is at work to build a better kingdom on earth.

110

So the lost language updated with images of our present time has the capability of giving us an instrument which in simple, vivid pictures can deal victoriously with the most complicated problems of our time. It can break through the false images which have divided us into warring nations. It can bring us happiness and satisfaction as we use it to describe a universe in which we are one humanity sailing through space on a fragile planet.

A NEW SENSE OF DESTINY
Chapter 16
"Therefore"

We search our days for purpose. Wanton and wasted days hang heavily in memory. There is something deep in the heart, which cries for greater "meaning" with the passage of the years. In answer to that inner cry, as we come to the last pages, we want to say, "therefore," that is... challenge the inner motivation with something that we must be or do. "I am come that you might have life, and that more abundantly," said Jesus, enticing us to fulfillment of our God-within.[59] Walter Pater, English essayist, heard the divine within as he eloquently spoke for that which is more than flesh, "How shall we pass most swiftly from point to point and be present always at the focus where the greatest number of vital forces unite in the purest energy? To burn always with this hard, gemlike flame, to maintain this ecstasy, is success in life."[60]

Through hundreds of years thousands of pilgrims seeking an answer to the purpose for their lives have found themselves walking up the path to the main entrance doors of Chartres cathedral. Looking at the typanum above the central door they have seen the dynamic figure of Jesus the Christ surrounded by the symbols of the four evangelists gazing down upon them. An interplay between the sculpture and the divine heart of the pilgrim begins a moment of true worship... the inner voice responding to the Divine.

Such a perfect channel was the Nazarene for the vibrations of the ultimate that the course of humanity on planet earth was fantastically lifted by his presence. To be open to him... to let his spirit be our spirit... this for humans can cause us to be always "at the focus where the greatest number of vital forces unite in purest energy." But it is as hard for us to apprehend the fullness of Christ as it is to look long into the sun with naked eyes. It is easier to study at length the light of God through one of the four elements, air, fire, earth or water. In each of these elements the total energy is stepped down, as through an electrical transformer, to a level of power we can handle.

Furthermore, when we ponder upon it, we realize that the message of the signs of the zodiac is that each of us is unique. As persons born in a particular place in a special time we are relieved of trying to do all things everywhere at once. Not one of us is called to be Atlas carrying the entire burden of the earth on our shoulders alone. All that is asked of us is to be the best we can be with the talents which are ours. Removing the burden of trying to be more than we could ever be capable of, we can become relaxed, so at ease that we may begin to sense the presence of the eternal in the midst of our busy days. In this peaceful state of mind, we can function at optimum capability.

Arnold Mindell of the Jung Institute, Zurich, reminds us that all that is required of each human being is to fulfill our personal potential in our time and space. He presents his thought in the simple, expressive language of symbolism. "You have noticed, I am sure, that people repeatedly meet with old problems regardless of what sort of psychotherapy they use. The happiest of them are not the ones who have made birch trees out of maple trees, who have solved their problems or changed themselves but the ones who got birch saplings to grow respectfully into birch trees. Their goal was the never ending process of unfolding."[61]

We have demonstrated how each of the gospels was written in one of the four elemental styles. Then, knowing ourselves as air, fire, earth or water we can turn to that gospel which is most appropriate to our manner of expression. Let us read its pages slowly, let our imagination dream the scenes in all their fullness of life. In this way we can sense the power of the Creator in that manner which for us is most easily understood. Then let us meditate on how our personal life can be used to its maximum potential in the service of the cosmos. How may our talents best unfold for the benefit of a needy humanity balanced precariously in this moment of time on planet earth?

"Therefore"

MATTHEW, THE FIRST EVANGELIST
the divine in the style of human intelligence

    The Thinker... the one who must establish the interrelationship of ideas. "There must be a reason." The universe has a plan; this I seek to know.

As I gaze on this figure with the aspect of God as mind, I know that I have been given the mental capacity to solve the problems which have seemed to be more than I can understand. At this moment in history with the finest schools and universities, with the wealth of libraries giving us knowledge on thousands of subjects, with the abilities of computer networks to supply us quickly with data, our personal capacity to solve the formerly impossible is the greatest in human history.

Standing unafraid before the world's most baffling problems, I have the talent of mind, to understand and to solve whatever might come upon me. I thank God for the gift of mind, and pray that I shall not be lax in using it to full capacity.

MARK, THE SECOND EVANGELIST
the divine in the style of a lion

That one who to be alive must be a part of a chain of energy… the one who initiates action… who provides on-going power for the social order… the one who vitalizes ever-new activity.

As I look upon this figure with the aspect of God as power, I need fear no weakness of heart. When I feel crushed, broken in spirit, so helpless that the smallest task seems too much to try, I can receive energy as a lion to get up and do what must be done. Even as Peter resonated to the power in Jesus so can I draw upon lion-like sources of strength from the God within me. With all the talents of my individual person I remain limp without the vital force, the driving energy of the Leo-Christ who commanded the disciples to follow him, preached with power, drove out evil demons and healed the sick in a moment. When weary of life's trials I thank God for the one who can always renew the power to fight again.

LUKE, THE THIRD EVANGELIST
the divine in the style of an ox

The one who must put life to practical use…
ideas and energies brought down to earth… love of beauty,
sensual, appreciative of color, form, music. As tillers of the soil,
workers in the factories, butchers, bakers and grocery store clerks,
the ones who make it possible to live on planet earth.

"Blessed are the meek, for they shall inherit the earth."[62] As we look on this Christ, of the earth, born in the stall of animals, in Bethlehem "the House of Bread," raised as a carpenter, let us never scorn those who work humbly at the most basic tasks. We give thanks for all those sincere persons who do and dare to save the beautiful planet which is our home. For those who would keep clean the air, the water and soil we must be grateful. For the ones who feed the hungry and clothe the naked we are ever thankful.

JOHN, THE FOURTH EVANGELIST
the divine in the style of an eagle

*The mystic who blends a spiritual interaction
with the material… emotions, desires, beliefs of the heart…
search for the ultimate… unity of the present with the eternal…
the whole person at one with God.*

Can we see ourselves as citizens of two worlds – material and spiritual – in constant interchange?

"Truly, truly, I say to you, you will see heaven opened, and the angels of God ascending and descending upon the Son of Man."[63]

Looking to the brave prophets of old, many of whom died as martyrs yet continue to inspire and guide us from spirit, the author of The Letter to the Hebrews could say, "... since we are surrounded by so great a cloud of witnesses, let us also lay aside every weight and sin which clings so closely, and let us run with perseverance the race that is set before us."[64]

Guided and inspired from the spiritual universe, we find our true destiny in the material. This is the mystical insight of The Gospel According to John – the penetrating eye of the soaring eagle. To symbolically portray this message the builders of the churches often placed the Bible on a lectern in the form of a carving of an eagle.

Our title is A NEW SENSE OF DESTINY, but this sense is not really new; it was only lost for a time and is being found again. In this finding let there be joy. As we rediscover our sense of the sacred, the holy, may we know the joy felt by the father when the prodigal son returned with a new sense of right values and worthwhile direction, "... 'for this my son was dead, and is alive again; he was lost, and is found.' "[65]

A NEW SENSE OF DESTINY

At the close of the Bible in John's book of Revelation the four energy styles which have moved mankind throughout history were shown to the apostle in a vision. "And round the throne, on each side of the throne, are four living creatures, full of eyes in front and behind: the first living creature like a lion, the second living creature like an ox, the third living creature like the face of a man and the fourth living creature like a flying eagle. And the four living creatures, each of them with six wings, are full of eyes all round and within, and day and night they never cease to sing.

'Holy, holy, holy, is the Lord God Almighty,
who was and is and is to come!' "[66]

May those who read herein find a joyful rediscovery of who they are and what the fulfillment of their destiny might be.

notes

1. *Holy Bible,* Revised Standard Version, Thomas Nelson and Sons, I Corinthians 13:2

2. Faber Birren, *Color Psychology and Color Therapy,* University Books, pg. 216

3. Rodney Collin, *The Theory of Celestial Influence,* Samuel Weiser, Intro xi

4. Robert Blair Kaiser, *Psychology Today,* March '81, pg. 72

5. J.E. Cirlot, *Dictionary of Symbols, Philosophical Library,* Routledge & Kegan Paul, Intro. xxxv

6. Gregory Szanto, *The Marriage of Heaven and Earth,* Routledge & Kegan Paul, pg. 51

7. A.N. Didron, *Christian Iconography,* Frederick Ungar Publishing Co., **Vol. I,** pg. 4

8. ibid. pg. 3

9. ibid. pg. 6

10. *Holy Bible,* R.S.V., Matthew 2:6

11. ibid. Matthew 2:23

12. ibid. Matthew 6:19-23

13. ibid. Matthew 7:12

14. Algernon Charles Swinburne, *English Poetry of the Nineteenth Century,* F.S. Crofts & Co., A Ballad of Burdens, Stanza 4

15. *Holy Bible,* R.S.V., Mark 4:38-39

16. Wm. Shakespeare, *Hamlet,* Act III, Sc.1, line 56

17. T.S. Eliot, *Hollow Men, Familiar Quotations* –Bartlett, Garden City Publishing Co. pg. 899

18. *Holy Bible,* R.S.V. Luke 24:32

19. ibid. Matthew 5:5

20. ibid. John 1:1-3

21. J. Rumi, *Poet and Mystic, The Ascending Soul,* translated by R.A. Nicholson, Allen and Unwin, Ltd. Harper and Bros. pg. 103

22. *Holy Bible,* R.S.V. John 6:48

23. ibid. John 6:54

24. ibid. John 1:9

25. ibid. John 1:4

26. ibid. John 11:32-35

27. ibid. John 14:12

28. ibid. John 7:14-17

29. Minot J. Savage, *Earth's Common Things, Masterpieces of Religious Verse,* Harper and Brothers, Pg. 16

30. *Holy Bible,* R.S.V. John 17:20

32. ibid. John 3:6

33. ibid. John 17:22-23

34. J.E. Cirlot, *Dictionary of Symbols, Philosophical Library*, Routledge & Kegan Paul, pg. 339

35. ibid. pg. 337

36. *Holy Bible*, R.S.V., Ezekiel 1:4-10

37. ibid. Matthew 2:15

38. Caitlin and John Matthews, *The Western Way*, Routledge & Kegan Paul, pg. 24

39. Neil F. Michelsen, Box 16430, San Diego, CA 92116

40. Auguste Rodin, *Cathedrals of France*, Beacon Press pg. 73

41. George K. Lovgren, *The Art of Inner Seeing*, Foreword iii, Karl Bern Publishers, Sun City, Arizona

42. ibid. pg. 19

43. Dr. Abraham M. Rihbany, *The Syrian Christ*, Houghton Mifflin Co. pgs. 115-117

44. ibid. pg. 127

45. *Holy Bible*, R.S.V., Matthew 8:21

46. ibid. Matthew 8:22

47. *Holy Bible* K.J., Exodus 20:12

48. *Holy Bible*, R.S.V., Isaiah 2:4

49. S. Radhakrishnan, *Eastern Religions and Western Thought*, Preface viii, Oxford University Press, Ely House, London

50. Hans Selye, *Stress Without Distress*, Signet Book, pg. 137

51. ibid. pg. 82

52. Kenneth R. Pelletier, *Toward a Science of Consciousness*, Delta Book, pg. 24

53. Dane Rudhyar, *The Astrology of Personality*, Doubleday, pg. 76

54. Rob Hand, *Celestial Influences 1985*, Quicksilver Productions, Ashland, Oregon

55. Margaret Mead, *Peter's Quotations, Ideas for Our Time*, Wm. Morrow & Co. pg. 171

56. ibid. Dr. Paul R. Ehrlich, pg. 388

57. Dane Rudhyar, *The Astrology of Personality*, Doubleday, pg. 77

58. David Bohm, *Wholeness and the Implicate Order*, Ark Paperbacks, Routledge & Kegan Paul, pg. 209

59. *Holy Bible*, R.S.V., John 10:10

60. Walter Pater, *The Renaissance. The Great Quotations*, George Seldes, Castle Books, pg. 552

61. Arnold Mindell, *RIVER'S WAY*, Routledge & Kegan Paul, pg. 121

62. *Holy Bible*, R.S.V., Matthew 5:5

63. ibid. John 1:51

64. ibid. Hebrews 12:1

65. ibid. Revelation 4:6-8